shar pei

understanding and
caring for your breed

Written by
Rosalind Hammond

shar pei

understanding and
caring for your breed

Written by
Rosalind Hammond

Pet Book Publishing Company

The Old Hen House, St Martin's Farm, Zeals, BA12 6NZ,
United Kingdom.

Printed and bound in South Korea.

ISBN: 978 1 910488 27 0
ISBN: 1 910488 27 5

Acknowledgements

Photography: Tracy Morgan

www.animalphotgrapher.co.uk

Contents

Introducing the Shar Pei

Beautiful or ugly? The Shar Pei, with a head shaped like a hippopotamus, is the *jolie laide* of the dog world; there are those who admire his unique appearance, and those who just don't see what all the fuss is about! However, looks are not everything, and the Shar Pei boasts a very individual personality to go with his distinctive appearance.

Characteristics

The Chinese Shar Pei was little known outside his native home until the 1970s when the breed was introduced to the USA.

Bred as a guard, employed as an all-purpose farm dog, and later as a fighting dog, it was the breed's highly unusual appearance which caught the public's

imagination. As puppies, Shar Pei have loose folds of skin or wrinkles, which become far less evident in adulthood. But Shar Pei puppies are irresistibly photogenic, and it was not long before they were featured in numerous advertising campaigns –the more wrinkly the puppy, the more the public – and the media – liked it!

As we shall see, this was to the detriment of the breed (see Developing the Breed, page 18) which has so much more to offer.

This ancient breed is built to be active and agile; he has a strong, muscular, compact body, which allows him to move freely, and with considerable endurance.

He thrives on a regime of physical exercise, and although he is medium-sized, which means he will fit in with most households, he is better suited to a more energetic family.

This is a breed with a number of distinctive features. As well as his peculiar hippopotamus head, his tiny ears and loose folds of skin, he has a scowling expression which is much prized in the show world. He also has a blue/black tongue, an unusual trait that he shares with the Chow Chow, another breed with Chinese origins.

*The blue tongue is a
feature of the breed.*

The Shar Pei has a remarkably harsh coat, which can be a short and bristly 'horse' coat or a slightly longer 'brush' coat. Occasionally a Shar Pei with a longer, thicker 'bear' coat will appear in a litter, but this type of coat is not recognised in the show ring. In terms of colour, the Shar Pei can be any solid colour, except white.

Living with a Shar Pei

What can you expect if you bring a Shar Pei into your home? This is a dog with a regal bearing, and this fits in with his character.

He is self-assured, and can appear slightly aloof with strangers. But in his family, he is exceptionally loyal and loving. He has a streak of independence, matched with a degree of stubbornness, so training must be tailored to suit him.

His background as an all-round farm dog means that he has a relatively high hunting instinct, but if care is taken he can learn to live with cats and other small animals. The Shar Pei was also used as a fighting dog in his native home, and although this part of his history is long gone, he can be assertive around other dogs.

For this reason, early socialisation around dogs of sound temperament should be considered essential.

He will live happily with other dogs in the family, as long as initial interactions are carefully supervised.

Health and longevity

Unscrupulous breeding of Shar Pei to cash in on their unique appearance has led to a number of health issues which include eye, skin, and respiratory conditions, as well as an autoimmune disease known as Shar Pei fever (see page 186).

Dedicated breeders are striving to eliminate these problems from their breeding programmes, and it is essential that any attempt to exaggerate breed characteristics, such as excessive wrinkles, should be heavily penalised.

A well-bred Shar Pei, who is given the correct diet, care and exercise, has a life expectancy of about 10 years.

Summing up

The Shar Pei is a fascinating breed, in terms of looks and personality.

However, he does have particular needs and is better suited to an experienced dog owner who will enjoy training and socialising him, and will get the very best from this wonderful dog.

Tracing back in time

The Shar Pei is an ancient Chinese breed and over the centuries these dogs have been used for many purposes before being established as companion dogs.

Han dynasty

The first evidence of Shar Pei type dogs dates back to the Han Dynasty, which lasted from 206 BC to 220 AD.

Clay figurines resembling dogs have been found in many burial sites in the Kwun Tung province, which is located near Canton in the south of China.

The models show a short-legged, square-shaped dog, with a curling tail and a scowling expression which bear a strong resemblance to today's Shar Pei.

The breed's ancestors remain a mystery, but it seems likely that the Chow Chow is in his genetic make up and the Mastiff - most particularly the

Tibetan Mastiff – could also have played a part.

The blue-black tongue of both the Shar Pei and the Chow Chow is a rarity in the dog world and indicates there is a strong link between the two breeds.

Fighting dogs

The Shar Pei is famed for his skin folds and wrinkles and there is a theory that these came about because he was bred down from giant-sized breeds.

This theory is supported by the Shar Pei's rapid growth rate from puppyhood to adulthood (see page 100).

What is certain is that Shar Pei type dogs were used for fighting during the Han Dynasty, and they proved to be formidable opponents.

Equipped with powerful jaws, and plenty of courage, a Shar Pei could hold his opponent and inflict considerable injury.

His harsh, bristly coat was uncomfortable to hold, and his loose skin folds meant he had the flexibility to break his opponent's hold during a fight. Even his small ears proved to be an asset – they were so tiny, no dog could get hold of them.

The Shar Pei's ability to relate to people, and to use his own initiative, meant he was used as a multipurpose farm dog, for hunting game – usually wild pig – and as a watch dog to guard his home and family.

The trail goes cold

Just as we feel we are getting to grips with the Shar Pei's history, we lose track of his story. We know that war and famine in China over several centuries took its toll on everyday life and dog ownership declined dramatically.

But the on-going history of the breed can only be a matter of speculation due to lack of documentary evidence.

This was exacerbated by the actions of the Emperor Yuan in the Mongol Dynasty which dates from 1260-1368.

Knowing he was about to be killed, he set fire to 140,000 ancient books rather than letting them fall into the wrong hands, thus destroying most of his country's cultural heritage.

Developing the breed

Historically, there has always been trade links between the East and the West, so it could well be that dogs of Chinese origin found their way to the West.

It was customary for emperors and heads of state to exchange gifts, and the Shar Pei may have been offered up as something uniquely Chinese.

The breed continued to exist in small numbers in China until the onset of communist rule which marked another dramatic change in its history.

Communist rule

China was taken over by the Communist Party in the 1940s and under the leadership of Mao Tse-tung the country underwent radical and devastating changes.

The Communist doctrine was absolute and there were decrees controlling every aspect of life. Owning a pet dog was considered to be a capitalist luxury

and heavy fines were imposed on all offenders. Even worse, the canine population was exterminated in many towns and villages.

Thankfully there were pockets of the country that escaped this massacre, and small numbers of dogs survived in the distant countryside, while a few were smuggled to Hong Kong, Macao and Taiwan, islands off the Chinese mainland.

A new life in the West

The Shar Pei survived in such small numbers it was in danger of disappearing altogether, but a young Chinese businessman, Matgo Law took on the challenge of saving the breed.

He searched Hong Kong for Shar Pei, and founded his Down-Homes kennels, breeding with the best specimens he could find.

However, he knew that his efforts would not be enough. In a now famous appeal, he wrote an article in the American Dogs magazine in 1973, telling the story of the Shar Pei and begging American dog fanciers to help save "the rarest breed in the world" as listed in the Guinness Book of Records.

The response was immediate, and a trickle of Shar Pei came to the USA. They were widely varying in type, but it is reckoned that the entire Shar Pei population stems from the first 200 dogs that left Hong Kong at this time.

In 1974 the Chinese Shar Pei Club of America was founded, and the breed was officially adopted in its new home in the West.

Since that time breeders have made substantial changes to the Shar Pei in terms of its appearance, so that it now looks quite different from the original dogs from Hong Kong.

Exaggeration has crept in as dogs have become shorter, stockier and much more wrinkled. Fortunately, there has been a swing of the pendulum and the international Shar Pei, which is now owned and loved in many countries, is becoming a healthier animal.

The Shar Pei is an outstanding and unusual companion dog and, hopefully, his future is now assured worldwide.

What should a Shar Pei look like?

The Shar Pei is one of the most distinctive looking of all pedigree dogs with his strong, muscular body, his large head and tiny ears, and the facial wrinkles which give him a unique scowling expression. This is a breed for the specialist, so what should we be looking for in the ideal specimen?

If you speak to most Shar Pei owners they will tell you they have the perfect dog and, of course, they do. Pet owners are not looking for perfection as in the world of show dogs; they are looking for the dog that is perfect for what they want. As long as he is obedient, has a good temperament and is easy to live with, he is perfect in their eyes.

In the world of show dogs, the perfect dog does not and will never exist; every dog has his faults. All breeders can do is strive to produce a dog that is fit for function and adheres as closely as possible to the Breed Standard, which is the written blueprint describing what the breed should look like.

In the show ring, the judge does not compare dog against dog, but each dog against the Breed Standard. The dog that, in their opinion, comes nearest to the Standard, is the winner. However the Breed Standard is open to interpretation and because of this you won't necessarily get the same dog winning every time. As we have seen, the Shar Pei has been championed in the USA and the Western version of the breed is described in their Breed Standard.

The Kennel Cub in the UK has its own Breed Standard and, following recent controversy, it is now listed as a 'high profile' breed. This means that breeders were producing Shar Pei that were subject to exaggeration in terms of appearance and the resulting predisposition to inherited health conditions.

The emphasis is now on breeding dogs which are "fit for function", and any form of exaggeration – particularly in relation to excessive wrinkling, – is heavily penalised in the show ring.

General appearance

This is a medium-sized, compact, short-coupled dog that is square in build. Males are larger and more powerful than females.

The coat is harsh and bristly and there are loose wrinkles on the body and the head, which should not be excessive in the adult dog.

Temperament

The Shar Pei has a regal air; he is calm and has an independent turn of mind, but he is devoted to his human family.

Head and skull

The Shar Pei has a large head but it should remain in proportion with his body. The skull is flat and broad, but what is extraordinary is the large, broad muzzle which resembles that of a hippopotamus. When viewed from the front, the bottom jaw appears to be wider than the top jaw. The nose is large, wide, and preferably black. There should be moderate wrinkle on the forehead and cheeks. This is much more noticeable in puppies but in mature, adult dogs excessive wrinkling will be faulted in the show ring.

Eyes

The American Standard stipulates that the eyes should be small and sunken, whereas the KC Standard, which focuses on moderation, asks for medium-sized, almond-shaped eyes. However, both Standards demand the scowling expression which is a special feature of the breed.

Dark eyes are preferred, but amber and lighter coloured eyes are allowed in dogs with pale coat colours. Although there should be wrinkling above

Points of anatomy

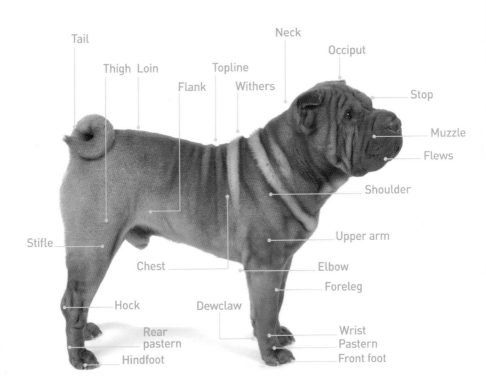

Tail

Thigh   Loin

Flank

Topline

Withers

Neck

Occiput

Stop

Muzzle

Flews

Shoulder

Upper arm

Stifle

Chest

Elbow

Foreleg

Hock

Dewclaw

Rear pastern

Wrist

Pastern

Hindfoot

Front foot

the eyes, it must not interfere with the function of the eyeball or the eyelid. Evidence of irritation of the eyeball or conjunctiva, or entropion (where the eyelids turn inwards), are severely penalised.

Ears

The Shar Pei has a big head, although it is in proportion to his body, but his small ears are a very distinctive feature.

They are relatively thick, equilaterally triangular in shape, and slightly rounded at the tip. Set high on the head, and well apart, the tips point towards the eyes. Prick ears are considered a major fault.

Mouth

The teeth are strong and should meet in a scissor bite, with the teeth on the lower jaw closely overlapping teeth on the upper jaw. The Shar Pei characteristic is the blue-black coloured pigmentation of the mouth: the tongue, the roof of the mouth, the gums and the flews (lips).

Dogs with amber or lighter-coloured eyes, which go with a paler coat colour, would be expected to have a lavender coloured tongue.

In the UK a pink tongue is considered undesirable, whereas in the USA it would disqualify a dog from the show ring. The Shar Pei has padding on his lower lip, but this should be moderate and should not interfere with the functioning of his mouth or teeth.

Neck

The neck is of medium length and is set well on the shoulders, allowing for a proud carriage of the head. There may be some loose skin under the neck but, again, this should not be excessive.

The American Standard is not so severe on this and allows for moderate to heavy folds of loose skin, plus abundant dewlap (fold of skin under the throat) and about the neck.

Forequarters

The shoulders are muscular, well laid back and sloping; the elbows should be close to the body. The forelegs are straight, moderate in length and should show good bone. The pasterns (shock absorbers on the front legs) are strong, flexible and slightly sloping. There should be no wrinkling on the legs in adult dogs.

Body

In terms of proportions, the height at the withers (the highest point of the shoulders) is approximately equal to the length measured from the point of

The scowling expression is a hallmark of the breed.

shoulders to the point of buttock. The depth of brisket (the front part of the body between the front legs and below the chest) is approximately half of the height at the withers.

The chest is broad and deep; the topline should dip slightly behind the withers and rise over a short, broad loin.

Adult dogs should have moderate wrinkling over the shoulders and at the base of the tail. Excessive skin on the body of mature dogs is highly undesirable.

Hindquarters

Strong, muscular and moderately angulated; the hocks (ankles) are well let down and there should be no sign of thickening or wrinkling.

Feet

These are compact and moderate in size. The toes should be well-knuckled.

Tail

This is rounded in shape, narrowing to a fine tip. The high tail set is a breed characteristic; a Shar Pei may carry his tail high and curving, curved right over, or in a tight curl.

The Shar Pei is muscular and square in build.

Movement/gait

This should be free, vigorous and balanced. A stilted gait is highly undesirable.

Coat

The Shar Pei does not have a glamorous coat in terms of length, but its texture is unique to the breed. It is extremely harsh, off-standing on the body and lying flatter on the limbs. In terms of length, it can be a short and bristly 'horse' coat (under 1.25cm/half an inch), or a longer, thicker 'brush' coat which is about 2. 5cm/1in in length. Both coat types are judged to be of equal merit. Most importantly, the Shar Pei is shown in his natural state and is never trimmed.

Colour

All solid colours are allowed, with the exception of white. There may be lighter shading on the back of the thighs and the tail.

Size

Both the American and the English Standard state that dogs should be larger than bitches but give an overall guide of 46-51cm (18-20in) at the withers. The American Standard gives a weight guide of 20-27kg (45-60lb).

Summing up

Although the majority of Shar Pei are kept as pet dogs and will never be exhibited in the show ring, it is important that breeders strive for perfection and try to produce dogs that adhere as closely as possible to the Breed Standard. This is particularly important in a 'high profile' breed such as the Shar Pei where exaggeration can lead to significant health issues.

The Shar Pei has a harsh-textured coat, which is a notable breed characteristic.

What do you want from your Shar Pei?

There are hundreds of pedigree dog breeds to choose from so how can you be sure that the Shar Pei is the right dog for you? Before you decide on a Shar Pei, you need to be 100 per cent confident that this is the breed that is best suited to your lifestyle.

Companion

If you want an exceptionally loyal companion who will watch over you and your family, look no further.

The Shar Pei may be reserved with those he does not know, but he saves all his love and affection for his family.

With sensible supervision, he will get on with children of all ages, and will act as both playmate and guardian.

For those getting on in years, the Shar Pei may not be the best choice.

Although he is medium-sized, he is compact and muscular which means he can be surprisingly strong, particularly in the case of males.

Obviously training, especially lead training, will result in a well behaved dog, but the growing up, adolescent period can be a trying time and may prove to be a step too far.

A routine of varied exercise should be considered essential for an adult dog, and you will need to spend a considerable amount of time on training and socialising, particularly during the first 12 months.

However, if you are reasonably active and have the time to devote to this exceptional breed, you will be rewarded with his unstinting devotion.

Watch dog

The Shar Pei was bred in part as a watch dog, and he remains highly alert, ready to sound a warning at the approach of strangers.

He is keen to guard his home and protect his family, but a well socialised Shar Pei will accept all newcomers with calmness and tolerance if you take the lead and make the decisions for him (see Social skills, page 120).

The Shar Pei is ready to protect both home and family.

Sports dog

There is no doubting the Shar Pei's intelligence, but whether it can be channelled into competitive sports is open to debate.

If you have the time and patience, you will certainly get there but you will need to tune into the Shar Pei mindset, and be creative in your training.

If you enjoy a challenge – and you find the right motivation and reward system – who knows what you can achieve? For more information, see Opportunities for Shar Pei page 152.

Show dog

In terms of showing, the Shar Pei is a relatively new breed as it was not known in the West until the 1970s.

In this short period of time, the demands, outlined in the Breed Standard, have changed and the emphasis is now on exhibiting healthy dogs, free from exaggeration, that remain typical of the breed.

Breeders are now focused on eliminating inherited health conditions from their breeding programmes, and only the very best of stock is exhibited in the show ring.

You will need to research pedigrees if you want to buy a show quality puppy.

What does your Shar Pei want from you?

A dog cannot speak for himself, so we need to view the world from a canine perspective and work out what a Shar Pei needs in order to live a happy, contented and fulfilling life.

There is no doubt that this is a significant phase in the breed's history, and if you get involved in the showing of Shar Pei, you could become instrumental in insuring the health and well being of future generations.

Time and commitment

First of all, a Shar Pei needs a commitment that you will care for him for the duration of his life – guiding him through his puppyhood, enjoying his adulthood,

and being there for him in his later years. If all potential owners were prepared to make this pledge, there would scarcely be any dogs in rescue. The Shar Pei is a home orientated dog; he loves his own special people and his role in life is to be close at hand, watching over them, having fun with them, and being included in family outings. If he is excluded, or if he is expected to spend long periods on his own, he will be thoroughly miserable. The Shar Pei is a proud dog, and he may not show his feelings by being vocal or destructive – the classic signs of separation anxiety – but he will close in on himself and suffer in silence, which would be a cause of deep concern for the caring dog owner. If you have to go out to work, or need to be away from home for more than four hours at a stretch, delay dog ownership until your circumstances change.

Practical matters

Grooming is straightforward with the short-coated Shar Pei, but you still need to pay attention to his basic care needs. All dogs should be routinely checked once a week to ensure they are in good health. Bear in mind that if you spot signs of trouble at an early stage, treatment is likely to be far more effective. The Shar Pei enjoys his exercise, and although he is not as energetic as some of the sporting and working breeds, he enjoys the stimulation of going to new places. If you have access to safe areas, he will relish the opportunity to use his nose and discover interesting smells, and he will also benefit from free running exercise.

Leadership

The Shar Pei takes his role as family companion/ watch dog very seriously, and this is one of the great pleasures of owning this exotic breed. However, you need to establish yourself in the role of leader so that your Shar Pei understands his place in the family circle. Yes, he is there to love and protect his family, but he must take the lead from you, meeting and greeting strangers with tolerance rather than suspicion. Do not allow your Shar Pei to be the decision-maker – that is your job. You need to spend time training him and socialising him so that he understands his role and what is required of him.

This does not mean that you have to be a domineering pack leader or, worse still, try to get your message over with harsh handling. A puppy learns best if you praise and reward the behaviour you want. He will then repeat it in the expectation of more rewards. It is important not to neglect this aspect of your Shar Pei's education. A happy dog is one that is content with his place in the family and understands where his boundaries lie.

Extra
considerations

Now you have decided that a Shar Pei is the dog of your dreams, you can narrow your choice so you know exactly what you are looking for.

Male or female?

Whether you get a male or female Shar Pei comes down to personal preference. Males are bigger and stronger than females, which may be a consideration, but differences in temperament are of greater significance.

All Shar Pei are individuals in their own right, but there are some gender traits that come to the fore. Most owners agree that the male Shar Pei is outstanding in terms of loyalty, but there is no doubt that females are loving and affectionate. Aggression is not a major problem in the breed, particularly if your Shar Pei is socialised with other dogs from an early age, but this trait may be more evident in males than in females. Owners have commented that a male Shar Pei is the same every day, whereas a female is prone to mood swings. She may be keen on fussing and petting one day, and the next she may feel more reserved and would rather do without the attention. This can be problematic if you have young children in the family who are not able to 'read' how a dog is feeling. However, the overriding temperament is sound, and with sensible management, both male and female Shar Pei will be trustworthy family companions.

If you opt for a female, you will need to cope with her seasons, which will start at any time from six months onwards and occur approximately twice-yearly thereafter. During the three-week period of a season, you will need to keep your bitch away from entire males (males that have not been neutered) to eliminate the risk of an unwanted pregnancy. Some owners also report that females may be a little moody and withdrawn during their seasonal cycle,

Many pet owners opt for neutering, which puts an end to the seasons, and has many attendant health benefits. The operation, known as spaying, is usually carried out at some point after the first season. The best plan is to seek advice from your vet.

An entire male may not cause many problems, although some do have a stronger tendency to mark, which could include areas such as the house. However, training will usually put a stop to this. An entire male will also be on the lookout for bitches in season, and this may lead to difficulties, depending on your circumstances.

Neutering (castrating) a male is a relatively simple operation, and there are associated health benefits. Again, you should seek advice from your vet.

Colour

The Shar Pei can be any solid colour, except white. Colours to choose from include: Red, Red fawn, Five-point red (reddish liver), also referred to as Red dilute, Black, Isabella (blue/liver), Cream, Blue, Brown, Cream dilute, Apricot dilute, Chocolate, Chocolate dilute, Lilac.

Dilutes can be found in all colours; it is accompanied with an absence of black pigmentation, amber eyes and a lavender tongue. Shading is a feature of all colours, with the exception of mahogany red.

More than one?

Owning a Shar Pei can be addictive and you may want to expand your dog population. With the Shar Pei, you need to consider this carefully.

Be very wary of a breeder who encourages you to buy two puppies from the same litter, as it is unlikely that the welfare of the puppies is their top priority. Most responsible breeders have a waiting list of potential purchasers before a litter is even born and have no need to make this type of sale.

If you do decide to take on a second Shar Pei wait at least 18 months so your first dog is fully trained and settled before embarking on a puppy. Bear in mind, some Shar Pei can have aggressive tendencies, and so relationships between dogs in the same household should never be taken for granted.

Colours range from cream to red fawn.

If dogs are introduced to each other carefully, they will learn to live in harmony, and there are many examples of same sexes (two males or two females) and mixed pairs (male and female) who get on well together.

However, a male and a female is probably an ideal combination. Obviously if you go ahead with this, one or both dogs will need to be neutered

An older dog

You may decide to miss out on the puppy phase and take on an older dog instead. Such a dog may be harder to track down, but sometimes a breeder will rehome a female when her breeding career is at an end so she will enjoy the benefits of getting more individual attention.

In some cases, the breeder may have run on a puppy as potential breeding stock and then found he/she is not suitable for this role, but will still make an excellent pet dog.

There are advantages to taking on an older dog, as you know exactly what you are getting.

But the upheaval of changing homes can be quite upsetting, so you will need to have plenty of patience during the settling in period.

Rehoming a rescued dog

Numerically, Shar Pei still count as a comparatively small breed and therefore it is unusual to find a Shar Pei in an all breed rescue shelter. However, breed clubs run their own rescue schemes, and this is where you will find dogs that have failed to thrive in their first homes. Sometimes a dog needs to be rehomed through no fault of his own, mostly when a family's circumstances change.

The reasons are various, ranging from illness or death of the original owner to family breakdown, changing jobs, or even the arrival of a new baby. However, there are cases where a Shar Pei has not received the training and socialisation he needs, and has become a 'problem' dog. As already highlighted, the Shar Pei is not a breed for the novice owner, and taking on a dog with behavioural problems is a major challenge and should only be undertaken by those who have the necessary experience and knowledge.

Regardless of the dog's previous history, you will need to give him plenty of time and be patient with him as he settles into his new home. It may take weeks, or even months before he becomes fully integrated in the family, but if all goes well you will have the reward of knowing that you have given a Shar Pei a second chance.

Sourcing a puppy

Your aim is to find a healthy Shar Pei puppy that has been reared with the greatest possible care. Where do you start?

A tried-and-trusted method of finding a puppy is to attend a dog show where your chosen breed is being exhibited. This will give you the opportunity to see lots of different Shar Pei.

The classes are divided between males and females, so you will get an idea of the difference in size between the sexes, and you will also see a variety of colours.

But when you look closely, you will also see there are different 'types' on show. They are all purebred Shar Pei but breeders produce dogs with a family likeness, so you can see which type you prefer.

When judging has been completed, talk to the

exhibitors and find out more about their dogs. They may not have puppies available, but some will be planning a litter, and you may decide to put your name on a waiting list.

Internet research

The Internet is an excellent resource, but when it comes to finding a puppy, use it with care:

- **DO** go to the website of your national Kennel Club. Both the American Kennel Club (AKC) and the Kennel Club (KC) have excellent websites which will give you information about the Shar Pei as a breed, and what to look for when choosing a puppy. You will also find contact details for specialist breed clubs (see below).

- Both sites have lists of puppies available, and you can look out for breeders of merit (AKC) and assured breeders (KC) which indicates that a code of conduct has been adhered to.

- **DO** find details of specialist breed clubs.

- On breed club websites you will find lots of useful information which will help you to care for your Shar Pei. There may be contact details of breeders in your area, or you may need to go through the club secretary. Some websites also have a list of breeders that have puppies available. The advantage of going through a breed club is that members will follow a code of ethics, and this will give you some guarantees regarding breeding stock and health checks.

If you are planning to show your Shar Pei you will need to find a breeder that specialises in show lines, and has a reputation for producing top quality dogs.

Remember that the health of the Shar Pei is a top priority so you are looking for a breeder who focuses on producing animals that are typical of the breed but without the exaggeration which has been so much to their detriment.

DO NOT look at puppies for sale.

There are legitimate Shar Pei breeders with their own websites, and they may, occasionally, advertise a litter, although in most cases reputable breeders have waiting lists for their puppies. The danger comes from unscrupulous breeders that produce puppies purely for profit, with no thought for the health of the dogs they breed from and no care given to rearing the litter. Photos of puppies are hard to resist, but never make a decision based purely on an advertisement. You need to find out who the breeder is, and have the opportunity to visit their premises and inspect the litter before making a decision.

Questions, questions, questions

When you find a breeder with puppies available, you will have lots of questions to ask. These should include the following:

- Where have the puppies been reared? Hopefully, they will be in a home environment, which gives them the best possible start in life.

- How many are in the litter?

- What is the split of males and females?

- What colours are available?

- How many have already been spoken for? The breeder will probably be keeping a puppy to show or for breeding, and there may be others on a waiting list.

- Can I see the mother with her puppies?

- What age are the puppies?

- When will they be ready to go to their new homes?

- Bear in mind puppies need to be with their mother and siblings until they are eight weeks of age otherwise they miss out on vital learning and communication skills which will have a detrimental effect on them for the rest of their lives.

You should also be prepared to answer a number of searching questions so the breeder can check if you are suitable as a potential owner of one of their precious puppies.

You will be asked some or all of the following questions:

- What is your home set up?

- Do you have children/grandchildren?

- What are their ages?

- Do you have a securely-fenced garden?

- Is there somebody at home the majority of the time?

- What is your previous experience with dogs?

- Do you already have other dogs at home?

- Do you want to exhibit your Shar Pei in the show ring?

- Do you have plans to compete with your Shar Pei in one of the canine sports?

The breeder is not being intrusive; they need to understand the type of home you will be able to provide in order to make the right match. Do not be offended by this.

The breeder is doing it for both the dog's benefit and also for yours. Steer clear of a breeder who does not ask you questions. He or she may be more interested in making money out of the puppies rather than ensuring that they go to good homes.

They may also have taken other short cuts, which may prove disastrous, and very expensive, in terms of vet bills or plain heartache.

Health issues

The Shar Pei does have a number of health issues, and it is vital that you check out the health history of the parents of the litter, and, ideally look back over several generations to discover if there is an incidence of conditions, such as entropion (an in-rolling of the eyelids), or other breed disposed conditions.

A responsible breeder should be completely honest about the health status of their breeding stock, as their aim is to produce healthy, typical puppies.

At present, there are no DNA tests for breed specific conditions in the Shar Pei, but parents should also be screened for both hip dysplasia and elbow dysplasia.

For information on inherited conditions, see page 180.

Puppy watching

A litter of Shar Pei puppies is totally irresistible. Rushing up to greet you, this band of miniature hippos all seem to say: "Take me home". However, you must try to put your feelings to one side so that you can make an informed choice.

You need to be 100 per cent confident that the breeding stock is healthy, and the puppies have been reared with love and care, before making a commitment to buy.

Viewing a litter

It is a good idea to have a mental checklist of what to look out for when you visit a breeder. You want to see:

- A clean, hygienic environment.

- Puppies who are out-going, friendly, and eager to meet you.

- A sweet natured mother who is ready to show off her puppies.

- Pups that are well covered, but not pot-bellied (which could be an indication of worms).

- Bright eyes, with no sign of soreness or discharge.

- Clean ears that smell fresh.

- No discharge from the eyes or nose.

- Clean rear ends – matting could indicate upset tummies.

- Lively pups that are keen to play.

It is important that you see the mother with her puppies as this will give you a good idea of the temperament they are likely to inherit. It is also helpful if you can see other close relatives so you can assess the type and temperament that the breeder produces.

In most cases, you will not be able to see the father (sire) as most breeders will travel some distance to find a stud dog that is not too close to their own bloodlines and complements their bitch.

However, you should be able to see photos of him and find out how he is bred, which will help you to make an informed decision.

A Shar Pei puppy looks especially enchanting with his frowning face and the folds of skin that ripple over his body.

The wrinkling reduces as a Shar Pei 'grows into' his skin, but bear in mind, it should not be excessive in puppyhood as related health problems could well ensue.

Companion puppy

In most cases, you will be wanting a Shar Pei purely and simply as a companion, and in this matter, your choice should be guided by the breeder. It is tempting to go for the pup that comes up to you first, or the one that makes you laugh as he chases his siblings.

But the breeder will have spent hours and hours watching the puppies as they have developed from newborns.

He/she therefore has an in-depth knowledge of how the puppies interact with each other, with other dogs in the family, how they relate to people, and how they cope with new experiences.

This is invaluable information when making the right match; the breeder will take into account your family set up and lifestyle and will help you to pick the most suitable puppy.

Show puppy

Do you have ambitions to exhibit your Shar Pei in the
show ring? If this is the case you need to make your
intentions clear to the breeder, so you can select
a puppy that has the potential to be successful in
the show ring. The aim is to find a Shar Pei that
will meet the stipulations set down in the Breed
Standard.

This is no easy matter when a puppy is only
eight weeks old, but an expert can make an
assessment, ensuring there are no obvious faults in
conformation and maybe finding that special spark
of showmanship, which can be a key ingredient
to success. If possible, recruit someone who is
experienced in the breed to view the puppies with
you, as they will be able to give their objective
opinion.

Basically, you are looking for a solidly built puppy,
which looks square in shape when viewed in profile.
The back should be fairly short and the legs should
be neither too long nor too short. At this stage the
head is fairly large but it should be in proportion
with the body. The ears should be small and pointing
towards the eyes.

Pay special attention to the eyes to ensure they are
free from defects (see page 183). There should be

prominent wrinkling on the forehead and cheeks, but this should not be excessive. The coat should feel harsh to the touch and should be either a short 'horse' coat or a longer 'brush' coat. A puppy with a longer 'bear' coat is not eligible for the show ring.

It takes an expert eye to evaluate show potential in a puppy.

A Shar Pei friendly home

It may seem an age before your Shar Pei puppy is ready to leave the breeder and move to his new home. But you can fill the time by getting your home ready, and buying the equipment you will need.

These preparations apply to a new puppy but, in reality, they are the means of creating an environment that is safe and secure for your Shar Pei throughout his life.

In the home

Nothing is safe when a puppy is about, and a Shar Pei puppy is no exception. Everything is new and exciting for a young puppy; it all needs thorough investigation – and this usually means testing with

mouth and teeth. One thing is certain – a free-ranging Shar Pei puppy cannot be trusted!

Remember, it is not only your prized possessions that are under threat; equally relevant is the damage a puppy can inflict on himself. Trailing electric cables are a major hazard so these will need to be secured out of reach.

You will need to make sure all cupboards and storage units cannot be opened – or broken into. This applies particularly in the kitchen where you may store cleaning materials, and other substances, which could be toxic to dogs.

There are a number of household plants that are poisonous, so these will need to relocated, along with breakable ornaments.

You may decide to declare upstairs off-limits and this is a sensible decision, particularly as negotiating stairs can be hazardous for a young puppy.

The best way of doing this is to use a baby gate; these can also be useful if you want to limit your Shar Pei's freedom in any other part of the house.

Owners with small children often use a baby gate to make sure that all dog interactions are supervised. This barrier works well, as your dog is separate but does not feel excluded from what is going on.

In the garden

Shar Pei do not tend to be escape artists, but there is always the exception to the rule so it is better to be safe than sorry. Your garden must be securely fenced; the height of the fencing should be approximately 1.52m (5ft). You also need to make sure there are no gaps, as there is always the chance a puppy will tunnel his way out! If you have a gate leading out of the garden it should have a secure fastening, and you would be advised to put up a sign, reminding visitors to shut the gate.

Some Shar Pei are enthusiastic gardeners, and will show no respect for your prized plants. It is bad enough to have your garden destroyed, but there is a serious risk that your Shar Pei could be in danger. There are a number of plants that are toxic to dogs so you need to check these out on the internet and remove them, or limit access to them before your puppy comes home. Swimming pools and ponds should be covered as most puppies are fearless and, although it is easy for a puppy to take the plunge, it is virtually impossible for him to get out unaided. You will also need to designate a toileting area. This will assist the house-training process, and it will also make cleaning up easier. For information on house-training, see page 140.

House rules

Before your puppy comes home, hold a family conference to decide on the house rules. You need to decide which rooms your puppy will have access to, and establish whether he is to be allowed on the furniture or not. It is important to start as you mean to go on. You cannot invite a puppy on to the sofa for cuddles only to decide in a few months' time that this is no longer desirable.

The Shar Pei is a strong-minded individual and he needs to know where his boundaries lie otherwise he will try his luck. However, if house rules are applied consistently, he will understand what is – and what is not – allowed, and will learn to respect you and co-operate.

Buying equipment

There are some essential items of equipment you will need for your Shar Pei. If you choose wisely, much of it will last for many years to come.

Indoor crate

Rearing a puppy is so much easier if you invest in an indoor crate. It provides a safe haven for your puppy at night, when you have to go out during the day, and at other times when you cannot supervise him. A puppy needs a base where he feels safe and secure, and where he can rest undisturbed. An indoor crate provides the perfect den, and many adults continue to use them throughout their lives.

Bear in mind the size your Shar Pei will be when he is fully grown, so buy a crate that is large enough for an adult dog. You may not have the same need to keep your Shar Pei out of mischief, but he will still appreciate having his own space where he can find peace and quiet. You will also need to consider

where you are going to locate the crate. The kitchen is usually the most suitable place as this is the hub of family life. Find a snug corner where the puppy can rest when he wants to, but where he can also see what is going on around him, and still be with the family.

Beds and bedding

The crate will need to be lined with bedding and the best type to buy is synthetic fleece. This is warm and cosy, and as moisture soaks through it, your puppy will not have a wet bed when he is tiny and is still unable to go through the night without relieving himself. This type of bedding is machine washable and easy to dry; buy two pieces, so you have one to use while the other piece is in the wash. If you have purchased a crate, you may not feel the need to buy an extra bed, although your Shar Pei may like to have a bed in the family room so he feels part of household activities. There is an amazing array of dog-beds to chose from – duvets, bean bags, cushions, baskets, igloos, mini-four posters – so you can take your pick! However, you do need to bear in mind that some beds prove irresistible as far as chewing is concerned, so delay making a major investment until your Shar Pei has outgrown the destructive, puppy phase.

Collar and lead

You may think that it is not worth buying a collar for the first few weeks, but the sooner your pup gets used to it, the better (see wearing a collar, page p134). A nylon lightweight collar is recommended, as most puppies will accept it without making a fuss. Be careful when you are fitting the collar that it is not too tight, but equally not too loose. This is quite tricky with a Shar Pei puppy as he has loose folds of skin around his neck; a good guideline is to make sure you can fit two of your fingers under the collar.

To begin with use a lightweight lead, making sure it has a secure trigger fastening. As your Shar Pei grows, you will probably need something more substantial.

There are plenty to choose from, but make sure the lead is made of a material, such as leather or soft nylon, which will not chafe your hands.

An extending lead can be a useful purchase as you can give your Shar Pei limited freedom when it is not safe or permitted to allow him off lead. However, you should never use it when walking alongside roads as an unexpected pull from your Shar Pei, resulting in the lead extending further than you intended, could have disastrous consequences.

ID

Your Shar Pei needs to wear some form of ID when he is out in public places. This can be in the form of a disc, engraved with your contact details, attached to the collar. When your Shar Pei is fully grown, you can buy an embroidered collar with your contact details, which eliminates the danger of the disc becoming detached from the collar.

You may also wish to consider a permanent form of ID. Increasingly breeders are getting puppies micro-chipped before they go to their new homes.

A micro-chip is the size of a grain of rice. It is 'injected' under the skin, usually between the shoulder blades, with a special needle. It has some tiny barbs on it, which dig into the tissue around where it lies, so it does not migrate from that spot.

Each chip has its own unique identification number that can only be read by a special scanner. That ID number is then registered on a national database with your name and details, so that if ever your dog is lost, he can be taken to any vet or rescue centre where he is scanned and then you are contacted.

If your puppy has not been micro-chipped, you can ask your vet to do it, maybe when he goes along for his vaccinations.

Bowls

Your Shar Pei will need two bowls; one for food, and one for fresh drinking water, which should always be readily available.

A stainless steel bowl is a good choice for a food bowl. Plastic bowls will almost certainly be chewed, and there is a danger that bacteria can collect in the small cracks that may appear.

You can opt for a second stainless steel bowl for drinking water, or you may prefer a heavier ceramic bowl, which will not be knocked over so easily.

Food

The breeder will let you know what your puppy is eating and should provide a full diet sheet to guide you through the first six months of your puppy's feeding regime – how much they should be eating per meal, how many meals per day, when to increase the amounts given per meal and when to reduce the meals per day. The breeder may provide you with some food when you go and collect your puppy, but it is worth making enquiries in advance about the availability of the brand that is recommended.

Grooming gear

The short-coated Shar Pei does not need a lot of grooming equipment, but coat care, and especially skin care, is very important in this breed.

For basic care you will need the following:

- Bristle brush: This type of brush can be used to work through the coat.

- Rubber curry comb: This is useful when a Shar Pei is shedding his coat as it helps to remove the dead hairs

- Nail-clippers: The guillotine type are easy to use.

- Toothbrush and toothpaste: Choose between a long-handled toothbrush or a finger brush, whichever you find easiest. There are flavoured canine toothpastes on the market, which your dog will enjoy.

- Ear wipes: These are easily obtained from most pet shops and generally come in a tub, which is re-sealable to retain moisture.

- Facial wipes: You will need these to clean between the folds of skin.

Toys

Shar Pei puppies can be very playful, and toys to help them through the chewing phase should be considered essential. But before you get carried away with buying a vast range of toys to keep your puppy entertained, you need to think about which are the safest.

Below: It is important to stick to the breeder's diet while your Shar Pei settles into his new home.

Plastic toys can be shredded, cuddly toys can be chewed, and toys where the squeaker can be removed should be avoided at all costs. If your Shar Pei ingests part of a toy, it could well result in an internal blockage, and this can be fatal.

The toys to choose should be made of hard rubber; a large, rubber 'kong' which can be stuffed with food is ideal. You can also buy tough, rope tug toys which are virtually indestructible. If you choose any other type of toy, make sure your Shar Pei is always supervised when he is playing with it.

Finding a vet

Before your puppy arrives home, you should register with a vet. Visit some of the vets in your local area, and speak to other pet owners that you might know, to find out who they recommend. It is so important to find a good vet, almost as important as finding a good doctor for yourself. You need to find someone with whom you can build a good rapport and have complete faith in. Word of mouth is really the best recommendation.

When you contact a veterinary practice, find out the following:

- Does the surgery run an appointment system?

- What are the arrangements for emergency, out-of-hours cover?

- What facilities are available at the practice?

- Do the vets in the practice have experience in treating Shar Pei? This is important as there are a number of health related issues which are peculiar to this breed.

If you are satisfied with what you find, and the staff appear to be helpful and friendly, book an appointment so your puppy can have a health check a couple of days after you collect him.

Some puppies are very confident, wanting to play straight away and quickly making friends; others need a little longer. Keep a close check on your Shar Pei's body language and reactions so you can proceed at a pace he is comfortable with.

First, let him explore the garden. He will probably need to relieve himself after the journey home, so take him to the allocated toileting area and, when he performs, give him plenty of praise.

When you take your puppy indoors, let him investigate again. Show him his crate, and encourage him to enter by throwing in a treat. Let him sniff, and allow him to go in and out as he wants to.

Later on, when he is tired, you can put him in the crate while you stay in the room. In this way he will learn to settle and will not think he is being abandoned.

Settling in

When you first arrive home with your puppy, be careful not to overwhelm him. You and your family will be hugely excited, but the puppy is in a completely strange environment with new sounds, smells and sights. This is a daunting experience, even for the boldest of pups.

It is a good idea to feed your puppy in his crate, at least to begin with, as this helps to build up a positive association. It will not be long before your Shar Pei sees his crate as his own special den and will go there as a matter of choice.

Some owners place a blanket over the crate, covering the back and sides, so that it is even more cosy and den-like.

Meeting the family

Resist the temptation of inviting friends and neighbours to come and meet the new arrival; your puppy needs to focus on getting to know his new family for the first few days.

Try not to swamp your Shar Pei with too much attention. This is a dog who likes to take life at his own pace, so give him a chance to explore and find his feet. There will be plenty of time for cuddles later on! If you have children in the family, you need to keep everything as calm as possible. The Shar Pei will make an outstanding family companion, but he needs to learn how to behave around children. Equally children need to respect the dog as a living animal; he is not a toy to be pinched and pulled, and he should never be teased.

It is also important that children learn when a dog should be left in peace. This applies particularly when a dog is eating or resting. If your Shar Pei goes to his bed or to his crate, he is saying: "do not disturb", and children must take this on board.

Bear in mind, it is easy for a puppy to become over-excited by raised voices, or by children running around and behaving unpredictably, and this can easily lead to mouthing and nipping.

The best plan is to get the children to sit on the floor and give each of them a treat. Each child can then call the puppy, stroke him, and offer a treat. In this way the puppy realises that it is not a free for all, and that he needs to interact with each child calmly and sensibly in order to get his treat.

If he tries to nip or mouth, make sure there is a toy at the ready, so his attention can be diverted to something he is allowed to

Below: Try not to overwhelm your puppy when he first arrives in his new home.

bite. If you do this consistently, he will learn to inhibit his desire to mouth when he is interacting with people.

Right from the start, impose a rule that the children are not allowed to pick up or carry the puppy. They can cuddle him when they are sitting on the floor. This may sound a little severe, but a wriggly puppy can be dropped in an instant, sometimes with disastrous consequences. If possible, try to make sure your Shar Pei is only given attention when he has all four feet on the ground. He will be surprisingly strong for his size so if he learns, right from the start, that jumping up is not rewarding, it will pay dividends later on.

Involve all family members with your puppy's day-to-day care; this will enable the bond to develop with the whole family as opposed to just one person. Encourage the children to train and reward the puppy, teaching him to follow their commands without question.

The animal family

A Shar Pei is not always the most sociable when it comes to interacting with other dogs, but good relations can be established, particularly if you work hard at supervising early interactions.

In an ideal scenario, introduce your resident dog to the newcomer at the breeder's home. This works well as the puppy feels secure and the adult dog does not feel threatened. But if this is not possible, allow your dog to smell the puppy's bedding (the bedding supplied by the breeder is fine) before they actually meet so he familiarizes himself with the puppy's scent. The garden is the best place for introducing the puppy, as the adult will regard it as neutral territory. He will probably take a great interest in the puppy and sniff him all over. Most puppies are naturally submissive in this situation, and your pup may lick the other dog's mouth or roll over on to his back. Try not to interfere as this is the natural way that dogs get to know each other.

You will only need to intervene if the older dog is too boisterous, and alarms the puppy. In this case, it is a good idea to put the adult on his lead so you have some measure of control. It rarely takes long for an adult to accept a puppy, as he does not constitute a threat. This will be underlined if you make a big fuss of the older dog so that he has no reason to feel jealous. But no matter how well the two dogs are getting on, do not leave them alone unless one is crated.

Feline friends

The Shar Pei has quite a strong hunting instinct and so care must be taken if you have a cat in the family. A moving cat is a big temptation so your puppy must learn right from the start that cats are not for chasing. You will need to supervise early interactions and progress step by step, making sure the pair are never left alone together until their relationship is fully established.

If your Shar Pei seems very focused on the cat, it may be easier to confine him to a carrier for the first couple of meetings so your puppy has a chance to make his acquaintance in a controlled situation. Keep calling your puppy to you and rewarding him so that he does not get obsessed with cat watching. You can then graduate to holding your puppy while the cat is free, again rewarding him with a treat every time he responds to you and looks away from the cat. When you allow your puppy to go free, make sure the cat has an easy escape route, just in case he tries to chase. This is an on-going process but all the time your Shar Pei is learning that he is rewarded for ignoring the cat. In time, the novelty will wear off and the pair will live in peace.

Feeding

The breeder will generally provide enough food for the first few days so the puppy does not have to cope with a change in diet – and possible digestive upset – along with all the stress of moving home.

Some puppies eat up their food from the first meal onwards, others are more concerned by their new surroundings and are too distracted to eat. Do not worry unduly if your puppy seems disinterested in his food for the first day or so. Give him 10 minutes to eat what he wants and then remove the leftovers and start afresh at the next meal. Obviously if you have any concerns about your puppy in the first few days, seek advice from your vet. If your Shar Pei seems to lose interest in his food, try feeding him in his crate where he can eat in peace and will not be so distracted. It is also advisable to work at your Shar Pei's food manners so he never feels threatened when he is eating and does not feel protective of his food bowl.

You can do this by giving him half his ration, and then dropping food around his bowl. This will stop him guarding his bowl and, at the same time, he will see your presence in a positive light. You can also call him away from the bowl and reward him with some food – maybe something extra special – which he can take from your hand. Start doing this as soon as your puppy arrives in his new home, and continue working on it throughout his life.

The first night

Your puppy will have spent the first weeks of his life with his mother or curled up with his siblings. He is then taken from everything he knows as familiar, lavished with attention by his new family – and then comes bed time when he is left all alone. It is little wonder that he feels abandoned.

The best plan is to establish a night-time routine, and then stick to it so that your puppy knows what is expected of him. Take your puppy into the garden to relieve himself, and then settle him in his crate.

Some people leave a low light on for the puppy at night for the first week, others have tried a radio as company or a ticking clock. A covered hot-water bottle, filled with warm water, can also be a comfort.

Like people, puppies are all individuals and what works for one, does not necessarily work for another, so it is a matter of trial and error. Be very positive when you leave your puppy on his own; do not linger, or keep returning; this will make the situation more difficult.

It is inevitable that he will protest to begin with, but if you stick to your routine, he will accept that he gets left at night – but you always return in the morning.

Rescued dogs

Settling an older, rescued dog in the home is very similar to a puppy in as much as you will need to make the same preparations regarding his homecoming. As with a puppy, an older dog will need you to be consistent, so start as you mean to go on.

There is often an initial honeymoon period when you bring a rescued dog home, where he will be on his best behaviour for the first few weeks. It is after these first weeks that the true nature of the dog will show, so be prepared for subtle changes in his behaviour.

It may be advisable to register with a reputable training club, so you can seek advice on any training or behavioural issues at an early stage.

Above all, remember that a rescued dog ceases to be a rescued dog the moment he enters his forever home and should be treated like a much loved member of the family.

Settling into a new home can be an exhausting business...

House training

This is an aspect of training that first-time owners dread, but if you start as you mean to go on, it will not be long before your Shar Pei understands what is required. This is a breed that has a reputation for being clean, and most are very easy to house train.

The key to successful house training is vigilance and consistency. If you establish a routine, and you stick to it, your puppy will understand what is required. Equally, you must be there to supervise him at all times – except when he is safely tucked up in his crate. It is when a puppy is left to wander from room to room that accidents are most likely to happen.

As discussed earlier, you will have allocated a toileting area in your garden when preparing for your puppy's homecoming. You need to take your puppy to this area every time he needs to relieve himself so

he builds up an association and knows why you have brought him out to the garden.

Establish a routine and make sure you take your puppy out at the following times:

- First thing in the morning
- After mealtimes
- On waking from a sleep
- Following a play session
- Last thing at night.

A puppy should be taken out to relieve himself every two hours as an absolute minimum. If you can manage an hourly trip out, so much the better. The more often your puppy gets it 'right', the quicker he will learn to be clean in the house. It helps if you use a verbal cue, such as "busy", when your pup is performing and, in time, this will trigger the desired response.

Do not be tempted to put your puppy out on the doorstep in the hope that he will toilet on his own. Most pups simply sit there, waiting to get back inside the house! No matter how bad the weather is, accompany your puppy and give him lots of praise when he performs correctly.

Do not rush back inside as soon as he has finished, your puppy might start to delay in the hope of prolonging his time outside with you. Praise him, have a quick game – and then you can both return indoors.

When accidents happen

No matter how vigilant you are, there are bound to be accidents. If you witness the accident, take your puppy outside immediately, and give him lots of praise if he finishes his business out there.

If you are not there when he has an accident, do not scold him when you discover what has happened. He will not remember what he has done and will not understand why you are cross with him. Simply clean it up and resolve to be more vigilant next time.

Make sure you use a deodoriser, available in pet stores, when you clean up, otherwise your pup will be drawn to the smell and may be tempted to use the same spot again.

Choosing a diet

There are so many different types of dog food on sale – all claiming to be the best – so how do you know what is likely to suit your Shar Pei?

This is a breed that grows rapidly in the first six months – many dogs are close to their adult size by this age. It is therefore essential to feed a high-quality, well-balanced diet during this important growing period.

Generally, an adult maintenance diet should contain 21-24 per cent protein and 10-14 per cent fat. Protein levels should be higher in puppy diets, and reduced in veteran diets. Shar Pei are prone to skin allergies, so it is advisable to opt for a diet that is based on natural ingredients.

When choosing a diet, there are basically three categories to choose from:

Complete

This is probably the most popular diet as it is easy to feed and is specially formulated with all the nutrients your dog needs. This means that you should not add any supplements or you may upset the nutritional balance.

Most complete diets come in different life stages: puppy, adult maintenance and senior, so this means that your Shar Pei is getting what he needs when he is growing, during adulthood, and as he becomes older. You can even get prescription diets for dogs with particular health issues.

Canned/pouches

This type of food, known as wet food, is usually fed with hard biscuit, and most Shar Pei find it very appetizing. However, the ingredients – and the nutritional value – do vary significantly between the different brands so you will need to check the label. The more natural wet foods contain rice rather than other cereals containing gluten, so select this type to avoid allergic reactions.

Bear in mind that wet foods, as their name indicates, often have a high moisture content, so you need to be sure your Shar Pei is getting all the nutrition he needs.

Homemade

Some owners like to prepare meals especially for their dogs – and it is probably much appreciated. The danger is that although the food is tasty, and your Shar Pei may appreciate the variety, you cannot be sure that it has the correct nutritional balance. If this is a route you want to go down, you will need to find out the exact ratio of fats, carbohydrates, proteins, minerals and vitamins that are needed, which is quite an undertaking. The Barf (Biologically Appropriate Raw Food) diet is another, more natural approach to feeding. This can work very well for the Shar Pei who is predisposed to skin disorders triggered by a food allergy. Dogs are fed a diet mimicking what they would have eaten in the wild, consisting of raw meat, bone, muscle, fat, and vegetable matter. There are now a number of companies that specialise in producing the Barf diet in frozen form, which will make your job a lot easier.

Feeding regime

When your puppy arrives in his new home he will need four meals, evenly spaced throughout the day. You may decide to keep to the diet recommended by your puppy's breeder, and if your pup is thriving there is no need to change. However, if your puppy is not doing well on the food, or you have problems with supply, you will need to make a change.

When switching diets, it is very important to do it on a gradual basis, changing over from one food to the next, a little at a time, and spreading the transition over a week to 10 days. This will avoid the risk of digestive upset.

When your puppy is around 12 weeks, you can cut out one of his meals; he may well have started to leave some of his food indicating he is ready to do this. By six months, he can move on to two meals a day – a regime that will suit him for the rest of his life.

Faddy feeders

If your Shar Pei is reluctant to eat, especially during the settling in period, it is tempting to try to pander to him. One look from those dark eyes is enough to melt your heart, stirring you to greater efforts to find a food that your Shar Pei will really like. At first you may add some gravy, then you may try some chicken...

The clever Shar Pei will quickly realise that if he holds out, tastier treats will follow. This is a bad game to play as not only will you run out of tempting delicacies, you will also be losing your Shar Pei's respect.

If your dog is turning up his nose at mealtimes, give him 10 minutes to eat what he wants, and then take up his bowl and give him fresh food at his next mealtime.

You need to find a diet that suits your Shar Pei's age and lifestyle.

Do not feed him treats in between meals. If you continue this regime for a couple of days, your Shar Pei will realise that there is no percentage in holding out for better food as it never materialises.

In most cases, this is just a 'trying it on' phase, and if you cope with commonsense, you will soon return to the status quo and your Shar Pei will be content with his normal rations.

If, however, your dog refuses all food for more than 24 hours you need to observe his behaviour to see if there are any signs of ill health, which may involve the need for a veterinary check up.

Bones and chews

Puppies love to chew, and many adults also enjoy gnawing on a bone. A raw marrow bone is ideal, but make sure it is always given under supervision

Rawhide chews are best avoided; it is all too easy for a Shar Pei to bite off a chunk and swallow it, with the danger of it then causing a blockage.

Ideal weight

In order to help to keep your Shar Pei in good health it is necessary to monitor his weight. Obesity is a major problem among the canine population, and a dog that is fed too much, often coupled with insufficient exercise, is likely to pile on the pounds. A dog that is carrying too much weight is vulnerable to many health issues; he has a poorer quality of life as he cannot exercise properly, and he will almost certainly have a reduced life expectancy.

When judging your Shar Pei's condition, look at him from above, and make sure you can see a definite 'waist'. You should be able to feel his ribs, but not see them.

If you are concerned about your Shar Pei's weight, get into the habit of visiting your veterinary surgery on a monthly basis so that you can weigh him.

You can keep a record of his weight so you can make adjustments if necessary.

If you are concerned that your Shar Pei is putting on too much weight, or equally if you think he is underweight, consult your vet, who will help you to plan a suitable diet.

Caring for your Shar Pei

Generally speaking, the Shar Pei is not a difficult dog to care for with his short coat and moderate exercise requirements. However, his unique skin folds means he does have special needs which you need to be aware of.

Coat care

As already highlighted, the Shar Pei has two basic coat types: a short, harsh-textured 'horse' coat, and a slightly longer 'brush coat', which should be no longer than 2.5cm (1 in) in length. There is no undercoat on either coat type. In addition, a Shar Pei may have a longer 'bear' coat, which resembles the coat length of a Chow Chow.

This coat type occurs when both parents carry a recessive gene. It is considered a major fault in the show ring and Shar Pei with bear coats cannot be exhibited. However, a bear-coated Shar Pei makes a perfectly good companion dog.

When a Shar Pei puppy arrives in his new home, he will not need much in the way of grooming, regardless of coat type. However, it is important to get your pup used to being handled. This will stand him in good stead if he grows a high maintenance coat, and even if his adult grooming needs are going to be relatively straightforward, this aspect of his care should not be neglected.

A grooming session gives you the opportunity to check your dog and to discover any minor problems, such as sore places, or any abnormalities, such as lumps and bumps which may need to be investigated. Remember, if you spot a problem early on, you increase the chance of an early diagnosis and successful treatment.

The first step is to get your puppy used to being handled so that he accepts the attention without resentment. Initially, he will wriggle and attempt to mouth you, but just ignore his protests. Hold him steady for a few moments, and reward him when he is still. A puppy needs to learn that it is OK to be touched all over; if you fail to do this, he may try to warn you off by growling, which could develop into more problematic behaviour.

Start by handling your puppy all over, stroking him from his head to his tail. Lift up each paw in turn, and reward him with a treat when he co-operates. Then roll him over on to his back and tickle his tummy; this is a very vulnerable position for a dog to adopt, so do not force the issue. Be firm but gentle, and give your Shar Pei lots of praise when he does as you ask.

The adult Shar Pei is low maintenance when it comes to grooming. Allocate a weekly slot to work through his coat with a bristle brush, which has the dual benefit of removing dirt and aiding circulation. As the Shar Pei does not have an undercoat, shedding, which usually occurs twice a year, is not a major issue.

At these times, you may want to use a rubber curry comb on the

If you handle your puppy from an early age, and reward him, he will learn to accept all aspects of routine care.

coat which helps to remove dead hairs.

Bathing should be kept to a minimum as excessive use of shampoo will destroy the natural harsh texture of the coat. If you want to freshen up your Shar Pei, use a damp cloth and give him a wipe over.

Skin folds and wrinkles

The Shar Pei is prone to skin problems, which may be the result of allergies (see page 179), but sometimes it is because moisture has been allowed to build up in the skin folds and wrinkles resulting in sore, 'wet' skin, which can then become infected. Keep a close check on your Shar Pei's facial wrinkles, wiping him clean after he has eaten, and making sure moisture does not build up. You can buy specially formulated powder, which helps to keep the skin dry. The skin folds on the body should also be checked on a regular basis.

Routine care

In addition to grooming, you will need to carry out some routine care.

Eyes

Check the eyes for signs of soreness or discharge. This is especially important with a Shar Pei who has small eyes which can be prone to infection. This may be where wrinkling interferes with eye function, but, hopefully, your Shar Pei will have been bred without this form of exaggeration.

If there is debris around the eye, you can use a piece of cotton wool (cotton) – a separate piece for each eye – for cleaning. However, if there is discharge from the eye, you should book a visit to the vet who can examine the eyes and prescribe the appropriate treatment.

Ears

Checking ears is essential with the Shar Pei. A feature of the breed is their small ears, but the downside of this characteristic is small narrow, ear canals which can be predisposed to infection. The problem is that debris collects in the narrow ear canals and it is not easy to keep them clean.

The best plan is to buy ear-cleaning fluid which is specially formulated for dogs, and squirt a little inside the ear.

Massage the ear from the outside, and then use an ear wipe or a wad of damp cotton-wool to clean them. Then repeat the same procedure with the other ear. Do not probe into the ear canal or you risk doing more harm than good. If the ear appears to be particularly dirty and foul-smelling, consult your vet who will prescribe the appropriate treatment.

Teeth

Dental disease is increasing among dogs so teeth cleaning should be seen as an essential part of your care regime.

The build up of tartar on the teeth can result in tooth decay, gum infection and bad breath, and if it is allowed to accumulate, you may have no option but to get the teeth cleaned under anaesthetic.

When your Shar Pei is still a puppy, accustom him to teeth cleaning so it becomes a matter of routine. Dog toothpaste comes in a variety of meaty flavours, which your Shar Pei will like, so you can start by putting toothpaste on your finger and gently rubbing his teeth. You can then progress to using a finger brush or a toothbrush, whichever you find most convenient.

Remember to reward your Shar Pei when he co-operates and then he will positively look forward to his teeth-cleaning sessions.

Nails

Nail trimming is a task dreaded by many owners – and many dogs – but, again, if you start early on, your Shar Pei will get used to the task you have to perform and will not fight against it.

The Shar Pei generally has black nails (as opposed to white) so you cannot see the quick, which is the vein that runs through the nail.

This makes nail trimming more difficult as you need to avoid cutting into the quick. If you do this inadvertently, it is not disastrous, but it will cause the nail to bleed profusely.

This will be uncomfortable for your Shar Pei, and he will remember it next time you attempt to trim his nails. The best policy is to trim little and often so the nails don't grow too long, and you do not risk cutting too much and catching the quick.

Nail-trimming does not need to be an ordeal...

If you are worried about trimming your Shar Pei's nails, go to your vet so you can see it done properly. If you are still concerned, you can always use the services of a professional groomer.

Exercise

The Shar Pei thrives on having a busy, interesting life, and exercise should be seen as an essential part of his daily routine. It is important to bear in mind that exercise meets both mental and physical needs. He needs to be kept fit and active, but he also needs the stimulation of exploring new places and investigating different smells.

When your Shar Pei is growing, exercise needs to be limited as joints are vulnerable. Playing in the garden will be sufficient to begin with, stepping up to short outings on lead, with the opportunity to let off steam, free running for 10 minutes or so.

Once your Shar Pei is fully grown, you will need to factor in a least one 30 minute walk a day, which can be a combination of lead walking and free running. This should be regarded as the minimum requirement. A Shar Pei will certainly appreciate two walks a day – and he will be more than happy to accompany you on longer treks when you have some free time.

Swimming is an excellent form of exercise – some Shar Pei love it, others would do anything to avoid getting wet! If you allow your dog to swim, make sure you choose a safe stretch of water where there is easy access in and out.

Playing games

This is a great way of providing physical exercise and mental stimulation. The Shar Pei can be playful, particularly in puppyhood.

This can fade away as your dog matures – but only if you give up playing with him. Try to sustain this form of interaction, which helps to establish a bond and enrich your relationship with each other.

If your Shar Pei is not interested in playing, but is a bit of a foodie, there is a 'game' you can play which will use his mental energies and make use of his sense of smell.

Once in a while, do not give your Shar Pei his food in a bowl but scatter it over a small area in the garden. Let your Shar Pei see what you are doing, and then encourage him to "find" his dinner.

There are few dogs who can resist this, and they will positively relish the task of seeking out their food.

The older Shar Pei

The majority of Shar Pei make it into double figures, but few will live into their teens.

It is inevitable that your Shar Pei will slow up as he gets older; you need to keep a close check to monitor when this change occurs as it will vary from dog to dog.

The older Shar Pei may sleep more and he may be reluctant to go for longer walks. He may show signs of stiffness when he gets up from his bed, but these generally ease when he starts moving.

Some older Shar Pei may have impaired vision, and some may become a little deaf, but as long as their senses do not deteriorate dramatically, this is something older dogs learn to live with.

If you treat your older dog with kindness and consideration, he will enjoy his later years and suffer the minimum of discomfort.

It is advisable to switch him over to a senior diet, which is more suited to his needs, and you may need to adjust the quantity, as he will not be burning up the calories as he did when he was younger and more energetic.

Make sure his sleeping quarters are warm and free from draughts, and if he gets wet, make sure you dry him thoroughly. Most important of all, be guided by your Shar Pei.

The Shar Pei needs to be exercised in both mind and body.

He will have good days when he feels up to going for a walk, and other days when he would prefer to potter in the garden.

If you have a younger dog at home, this may stimulate your Shar Pei to take more of an interest in what is going on, but make sure he is not pestered as he needs to rest undisturbed when he is tired.

Letting go

Inevitably there comes a time when your Shar Pei is not enjoying a good quality of life, and you need to make the painful decision to let him go.

We would all wish that our dogs died, painlessly, in their sleep but, unfortunately, this is rarely the case.

However, we can allow our dogs to die with dignity, and to suffer as a little as possible, and this should be our way of saying thank you for the wonderful companionship they have given us.

When you feel the time is drawing close, talk to your vet who will be able to make an objective assessment of your Shar Pei's condition and will help you to make the right decision.

This is the hardest thing you will ever have to do as a dog owner, and it is only natural to grieve for your beloved Shar Pei.

But eventually, you will be able to look back on the happy memories of times spent together, and this will bring much comfort.

You may in time, feel that your life is not complete without a Shar Pei, and you will feel ready to welcome new puppy into your home.

Social Skills

To live in the modern world, without fear and anxieties, your Shar Pei needs to receive an education in social skills so that he learns to cope calmly and confidently in a wide variety of situations.

The Shar Pei's history as both watch dog and fighting dog is in the distant past, but there may be some traits from this genetic background which occasionally come to the fore. For this reason, it is especially important to work on developing your Shar Pei's social skills so that he tolerates other dogs and does not feel the need to guard his family

Early learning

The breeder will have begun a programme of socialisation by getting the puppies used to all the sights and sounds of a busy household.

You need to continue this when your pup arrives in his new home, making sure he is not worried by household equipment, such as the vacuum cleaner or the washing machine, and that he gets used to unexpected noises from the radio and television.

To begin with, your puppy needs to get used to all the members of his new family , but then you should give him the opportunity to meet friends and other people that come to the house.

If you do not have children of your own, make sure your puppy has the chance to meet and play with other people's children – making sure interactions are always supervised – so he learns that humans come in small sizes, too.

Meet and greet

The Shar Pei has a firm belief that he belongs to his 'people'; he will show great love and loyalty to family members and will tend to be suspicious of those he does not know.

While it may be useful to own a dog that gives you warning when strangers are approaching, and it may be gratifying to have a dog that is protective of his home and family, you should not seek to encourage these tendencies.

They are part of a Shar Pei's heritage and, in moderation, there is absolutely nothing wrong with them. However, if they are unchecked – or even encouraged – you will find yourself in a situation when you dread visitors coming to the house.

As a puppy, a Shar Pei needs to learn how to meet and greet people who come to the house, allowing you to make the decisions. The best way of doing this is to supervise interactions until your Shar Pei has learnt the necessary social skills.

To begin with, recruit a friend who is experienced with dogs, to visit the house:

When the doorbell rings, attach a lead to your Shar Pei so he is under control, and arm yourself with some treats.

Before you open the door, make sure your Shar Pei is sitting quietly. Reward him with a treat for co-operating. Open the door and make sure your Shar Pei remains sitting down. Again, give him a treat, and talk to your visitor for a couple of minutes on the door step. If your Shar Pei is remaining calm, give a couple of treats to your visitor and allow your Shar Pei to take them. Do not rush this stage.

Make sure your Shar Pei is relaxed, and is ready to accept some attention from the visitor. You can then allow the visitor into your home. Keep practising this scenario with dog-friendly people before you introduce a complete stranger who may have no knowledge of dogs. It is better to keep your Shar Pei in his crate rather than attempting an unscheduled meeting, which may upset all the good work you have done. This process sounds long winded but it is well worth the effort. You are teaching social skills which will stand your Shar Pei in good stead for the rest of his life.

The outside world

When your puppy has completed his vaccinations, he is ready to venture into the outside world. As a breed, the Shar Pei is generally confident but there is a lot for a youngster to take on board, so do not swamp him with too many new experiences when

Do not rush the socialisation process. Give your puppy time to gain confidence so he welcomes new experiences.

you first set out. Obviously you need to work at lead-training (see page 136) before you set out on your first expedition. There will be plenty of distractions to cope with, so you do not want the additional problem of coping with a dog that is pulling or lagging on the lead.

So, hopefully, you can set off with your Shar Pei walking by your side on a loose lead. He may need additional encouragement when you venture further afield, so arm yourself with some extra special treats, which will give him a good reason to focus on you when required! Start socialising your puppy in a quiet area with light traffic, and only progress to a busier place when he is ready. There is so much to see and hear – people (maybe carrying bags or umbrellas), pushchairs, bicycles, cars, lorries, machinery – so give your puppy a chance to take it all in.

If he does appear worried, do not fall into the trap of sympathizing with him, or worse still, picking him up. This will only teach your pup that he had a good reason to be worried and, with luck, you will 'rescue' him if he feels scared. Instead, give a little space so he does not have to confront whatever he is frightened of, and distract him with a few treats. Then encourage him to walk past, using an encouraging tone of voice, never forcing him by yanking on the lead. Reward him for any forward movement, and your puppy will soon learn that he can trust you, and there is nothing to fear.

Dog to dog meetings

Your pup also needs to continue his education in canine manners, started by his mother and by his littermates, as he needs to be able to greet all dogs calmly, giving the signals that say he is friendly and offers no threat. This is especially important with a Shar Pei. In the past the breed were used as fighting dogs, and although this aspect of their temperament has largely been eradicated by selective breeding, it is still a part of the Shar Pei's genetic make up.

Some individuals will be happy to meet other dogs without any effort on your part, others may feel the need to be assertive. To play safe, every Shar Pei owner should focus on socialisation with other dogs, particularly during puppyhood and adolescence.

Try the following:

- Find a friend who has a dog with a bombproof temperament and visit their house. Allow the two dogs to play in the garden for 10 minutes or so. Do not prolong the game as you do not want your youngster to become over-excited or overwhelmed.

- Once the two dogs have had a few play-dates at home, go for a walk and allow them to exercise together off lead. They will interact with each other, but their focus will shift periodically, as they will be distracted by other sights and smells.

- Try to extend your Shar Pei's circle of acquaintance by finding other friends who have dogs of sound temperament. The more your Shar Pei practises meeting and greeting the better he will become at reading body language and assessing other dogs' intentions.

- Try to avoid meeting with strange dogs unless you are completely confident that your Shar Pei will not react adversely. It is much better to keep your Shar Pei on the lead rather than allow a dog of unsound temperament to upset him and ruin all your good work.

If you observe your Shar Pei's body language you will begin to understand his moods and intentions.

Training classes

A training class will give your Shar Pei the opportunity to work alongside other dogs in a controlled situation, and he will also learn to focus on you in a different, distracting environment.

Both these lessons will be vital as your dog matures. However, the training class needs to be of the highest calibre or you risk doing more harm than good. Before you go along with your puppy, attend a class as an observer to make sure you are happy with what goes on.

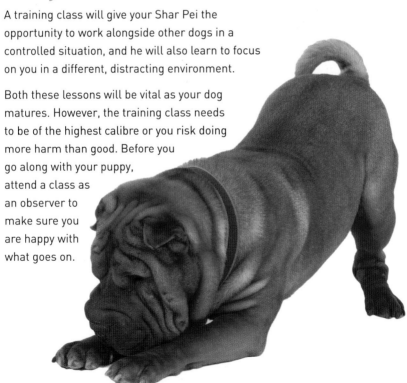

Training guidelines

The Shar Pei is a clever dog and is quick to learn. He will enjoy training sessions as he likes to use his brain, but make sure you keep rewarding, so your Shar Pei is motivated to co-operate and will enjoy spending quality time with you.

You will be keen to get started, but in your rush to get training underway, do not neglect the fundamentals that could make the difference between success and failure. You need to get into the mindset of a Shar Pei, working out what makes him tick and, equally, what makes him switch off. Decide on your priorities for training, set realistic targets, and then think of ways of making your training as positive, and as fun, as possible.

When you start training, try to observe the following guidelines:

- Choose an area that is free from distractions so your puppy will focus on you. You can progress to a more challenging environment as your pup progresses.

- Do not train your puppy just after he has eaten or when you have returned from exercise. He will either be too full, or too tired, to concentrate.

- Do not train if you are in a bad mood, or if you are short of time – these sessions always end in disaster!

Providing a worthwhile reward is an essential tool in training. You will probably get the best results if you use some extra special food treats, such as cheese or cooked liver. Some Shar Pei will work for a toy, but they are the exception rather than the rule.

If you decide to use a toy, make sure it is only brought out for training sessions so that it accrues added value.

- Keep your verbal cues simple, and always use the same one for each exercise. For example, when you ask your puppy to go into the Down position, the cue is "Down", not "Lie Down", Get Down", or anything else. Remember, your Shar Pei does not speak English; he associates the sound of the word with the action.

- If your dog is finding an exercise difficult, break it down into small steps so it is easier to understand. The Shar Pei has a stubborn side to his temperament, and if he becomes frustrated he may decide on a 'down tools' policy.

- Do not make your training sessions boring and repetitious. The Shar Pei is a thinking dog and he will withdraw his co-operation if he loses interest and there are no tangible rewards on offer.

- Do not train for too long, particularly with a young puppy that has a very short attention span, and always end training sessions on a positive note.

This does not necessarily mean getting an exercise right. If your pup is tired and making mistakes, ask him to do a simple exercise so you have the opportunity to praise and reward him.

You may well find that he benefits from having a break and will make better progress next time you try.

Remember that if your Shar Pei is rewarded for a behaviour, he is likely to repeat it – so make sure you are 100 per cent consistent and always reward the 'right' behaviour.

IFirst lessons

Like all puppies, a young Shar Pei will soak up new experiences like a sponge, so training should start from the time your pup arrives in his new home.

Wearing a collar

You may, or may not, want your Shar Pei to wear a collar all the time. But when he goes out in public places he will need to be on a lead, and so he should be used to the feel of a collar around his neck.

The best plan is to accustom your pup to wearing a soft collar for a few minutes at a time until he gets used to it.

Fit the collar so that you can get two fingers between the collar and his neck. Then have a game to distract his attention.

This will work for a few moments; then he will stop, put his back leg up behind his neck and scratch away at the peculiar itchy thing round his neck, which feels so odd.

Bend down, rotate the collar, pat him on the head and distract him by playing with a toy or giving him a treat. Once he has worn the collar for a few minutes each day, he will soon ignore it and become used to it.

Remember, never leave the collar on the puppy unsupervised, especially when he is outside in the garden, or when he is in his crate, as it is could get snagged, causing serious injury.

Walking on the lead

This is a simple exercise, but the Shar Pei can be a little stubborn, so it is a good idea to master the basics at home before venturing into the outside world where there is so much to distract him.

Once your puppy is used to the collar, take him outside into your secure garden where there are no distractions.

Attach the lead and, to begin with, allow him to wander with the lead trailing, making sure it does not become snagged. Then pick up the lead and follow the pup where he wants to go; he needs to get used to the sensation of being attached to you.

The next stage is to get your Shar Pei to follow you, and for this you will need some treats. To give yourself the best chance of success, make sure the treats are high value – cheese, sausage or liver – so your Shar Pei is motivated to work with you.

Show him you have a treat in your hand, and then encourage him to follow you. Walk a few paces, and if he is walking with you, stop and reward him. If he puts on the brakes, simply change direction and lure him with the treat.

Next introduce some changes of direction so your puppy is walking confidently alongside you. At this stage, introduce a verbal cue "Heel" when your puppy is in the correct position.

You can then graduate to walking your puppy outside the home – as long as he has completed his vaccination programme – starting in quiet areas and building up to busier environments.

Training strategy

The Shar Pei is a strong, muscular dog for his size, and any tendency to pull on the lead should be discouraged.

Your dog needs to learn, right from the start, that there is absolutely no percentage in pulling. Restrict lead training to the garden in the initial stages so you are working in an environment that is free from distractions.

Walk a few paces, being very aware of any tension on the lead. If you feel the lead tighten and your Shar Pei is attempting to get ahead of you, stop, change direction, and set off again.

Your Shar Pei needs to understand that pulling ahead has exactly the opposite effect to that which he wants. Rather than calling the tune, he has to co-operate with you.

Keep a good supply of tasty treats and remember only reward – with food and with verbal praise – when he is walking on a loose lead by your side.

The mistake made by many owners at this stage is to use the treats to lure the dog into position rather than rewarding him for the correct behaviour.

Keep training sessions short, and when you are ready to venture into the outside world, do not be too ambitious to begin with.

Build up the level of distraction and the duration of lead walking only when your Shar Pei is consistently showing the behaviour you want.

Work at your lead training at home so your Shar Pei knows the drill before you venture into the outside world.

Come when called

The Shar Pei is utterly devoted to his family, but there are times when he gets distracted. There are so many enticing smells out there you can appreciate that an instant response to the recall may not always be the preferred option.

The key to successful recall training is to start early, and to teach your Shar Pei to focus on you, regardless of temptations...

Hopefully, the breeder will have laid the foundations simply by calling the puppies to "Come" when it is dinnertime, or when they are moving from one place to another.

You can build on this when your puppy arrives in his new home, calling him to "Come" to welcome him; when he is in a confined space, such as the kitchen.

This is a good place to build up a positive association with the verbal cue – particularly if you ask your puppy to "Come" to get his dinner!

The next stage is to transfer the lesson to the garden. Arm yourself with some treats, and wait until your puppy is distracted. Then call him, using a higher-pitched, excited tone of voice. At this stage, a puppy wants to be with you, so capitalise on this and keep practising the verbal cue, and rewarding your puppy with a treat and lots of praise when he comes to you.

Now you are ready to introduce some distractions. Try calling him when someone else is in the garden, or wait a few minutes until he is investigating a really interesting scent. When he responds, make a really big fuss of him and give him some extra treats so he knows it is worth his while to come to you. If your puppy responds, immediately reward him with a treat.

If he is slow to come, run away a few steps and then call again, making yourself sound really exciting. Jump up and down, open your arms wide to welcome him; it doesn't matter how silly you look, he needs to see you as the most fun person in the world.

When you have a reliable recall in the garden, you can venture into the outside world. Do not be too ambitious to begin with; try a recall in a quiet place with the minimum of distractions so you can be assured of success

Do not make the mistake of only asking your dog to come at the end of his allotted exercise period. What is the incentive in coming back to you if all you do is clip on his lead, marking the end of his free time? Instead, call your dog at random times, giving him a treat and a stroke, and then letting him go free again. In this way, coming to you – and focusing on you – is always rewarding.

Coming back to you needs to be the most desirable option.

Stationary exercises

The Sit and Down are easy to teach, and mastering these exercises will be rewarding for both you and your Shar Pei. They are useful in a wide variety of situations and ensure that you always have a measure of control.

Sit

The best method is to lure your Shar Pei into position, and for this you can use a treat or his food bowl.

Hold the reward (a treat or food bowl) above his head. As he looks up, he will lower his hindquarters and go into a sit.

Practise this a few times and when your puppy understands what you are asking, introduce the verbal cue, "Sit".

When your Shar Pei understands the exercise, he

will respond to the verbal cue alone, and you will not need to reward him every time he sits.

However, it is a good idea to give him a treat on a random basis when he co-operates to keep him guessing!

Down

This is an important lesson, and can be a lifesaver if an emergency arises and you need to bring your Shar Pei to an instant halt.

You can start with your dog in a Sit or a Stand for this exercise. Stand or kneel in front of him and show him you have a treat in your hand. Hold the treat just in front of his nose and slowly lower it towards the ground, between his front legs.

As your Shar Pei follows the treat he will go down on his front legs and, in a few moments, his hindquarters will follow. Close your hand over the treat so he doesn't cheat and get the treat before he is in the correct position.

As soon as he is in the Down, give him the treat and lots of praise. Keep practising, and when your Shar Pei understands what you want, introduce the verbal cue "Down".

As with all training, once your Shar Pei has mastered an exercise take it to different locations – the garden or the park, for example. Unlike humans, dogs have to learn to generalise so that they understand and respond correctly to an instruction regardless of a change in environment

With practice, your Shar Pei will respond instantly to the verbal cue, "Down".

Control exercises

These exercises are not the most exciting, but they are especially important for a Shar Pei who needs to respect you, and to understand that he will be rewarded for making the right decision.

Wait

This exercise teaches your Shar Pei to "Wait" in position until you give the next command. It differs from the Stay exercise, where he must stay where you have left him for a more prolonged period. The most useful application of "Wait" is when you are getting your dog out of the car and you need him to stay in position until you clip on his lead.

Start with your puppy on the lead to give you a greater chance of success. Ask him to "Sit", then stand in front him. Step back one pace, holding

your hand, palm flat, facing him. Wait a second and then come back to stand in front of him. You can then reward him and release him with a word, such as "OK".

Practise this a few times, waiting a little longer before you reward him, and then introduce the verbal cue "Wait".

You can reinforce the lesson by using it in different situations, such as asking your Shar Pei to "Wait" before you put his food bowl down.

Stay

You need to differentiate this exercise from the Wait by using a different hand signal and a different verbal cue.

Start with your Shar Pei in the Down, as he is most likely to be secure in this position. Stand by his side and then step forwards, with your hand held back, palm facing the dog.

Step back, release him, and then reward him. Practise until your Shar Pei understands the exercise and then introduce the verbal cue "Stay".Gradually increase the distance you can leave your puppy, and increase the challenge by walking around him – and even stepping over him – so that he learns he must "Stay" until you release him.

Leave

A response to this verbal cue means that your Shar Pei will learn to give up a toy on request, and it follows that he will give up anything when he is asked, which is very useful if he has a forbidden object. This not simply a matter of obeying the verbal cue to "Leave"; it is establishing the status quo where you are the decision-maker and your Shar Pei is ready to co-operate with you.

The "Leave" command can be taught quite easily when you are first playing with your puppy. As you gently, take a toy from his mouth, introduce the verbal cue, "Leave", and then praise him.

If he is reluctant, swap the toy for another toy or a treat. This will usually do the trick.

Do not try to pull the toy from his mouth if he refuses to give it up, as you will make the situation confrontational.

Let the toy go 'dead' in your hand, and then swap it for a new toy, or a really high-value treat so this becomes the better option.

Remember to make a big fuss of your Shar Pei when he does as you ask so that he learns that co-operation is always the best – and most rewarding–option

Opportunities for Shar Pei

The Shar Pei has a brain and he will relish the chance to use it. However, he also has a mind of his own, which can make training more challenging. Working with your dog is an enriching experience – even if it is no more than teaching tricks. Think about your dog's need for mental stimulation; try to find something he enjoys doing, so you can spend quality time training him and interacting with him.

Good Citizen Scheme

The Kennel Club Good Citizen Scheme was introduced to promote responsible dog ownership, and to teach dogs basic good manners.

In the US there is one test; in the UK there are four award levels: Puppy Foundation, Bronze, Silver and Gold.

Exercises within the scheme include:

- Walking on lead
- Road walking
- Control at door/gate.
- Food manner
- Recall
- Stay
- Send to bed
- Emergency stop.

Agility

In Agility, the dog completes an obstacle course under the guidance of his owner. You need a good element of control, as the dog completes the course off the lead.

In competition, each dog is assessed on both time and accuracy. The dog that completes the course with the fewest faults, in the fastest time, wins the class.

The obstacles include an A-frame, a dog-walk, weaving poles, a seesaw, tunnels, and jumps. There is absolutely no reason why the Shar Pei, who has an active build and an alert mind, cannot do well in this discipline. Maybe more Shar Pei owners should give it a try and discover what fun it is for both dog and handler!

Competitive obedience

This is a sport where you are assessed as a dog and handler, completing a series of exercises including heelwork, recalls, retrieves, stays, sendaways and scent discrimination.

The Shar Pei is more than capable of competing in this discipline, but make sure training is fun, and you do not put too much pressure on your dog. The Obedience exercises are relatively simple to begin with, involving heelwork, a recall and stays in the lowest class, and, as your progress through, more exercises are added, and the aids you are allowed to give are reduced.

To achieve top honours in this discipline requires intensive training as precision and accuracy are of paramount importance. However, you must guard against drilling your Shar Pei, as he will quickly lose motivation.

Rally O

If you do not want to get involved in the rigours of Competitive Obedience, you may find that a sport called Rally O is more to your liking.

This is loosely based on Obedience, and also has a few exercises borrowed from Agility when you get to the highest levels. Handler and dog must complete a course, in the designated order, which has a variety of different exercises that could number from 12 to 20. The course is timed and the team must complete within the time limit that is set, but there are no bonus marks for speed.

The great advantage of Rally O is that it is very relaxed, and anyone can compete; indeed, it has proved very popular for handlers with disabilities, as they are able to work their dogs to a high standard and compete on equal terms.

Showing

The Shar Pei has a relatively short history in the show world and in the early years the number of entries in shows was very small.

However, this exotic breed from the East has grown in popularity among breeders and exhibitors and showing is now highly competitive.

To prepare for the show ring, you need to train your Shar Pei to stand in a show pose, to be examined by a judge, and to move correctly.

Ringcraft classes will teach you how to do this, and will also give you a good grounding in show etiquette. It also provides an excellent opportunity to socialise your Shar Pei with other dogs.

Heelwork to music

Also known as Canine Freestyle, this activity is becoming increasingly popular. Dog and handler perform a choreographed routine to music, allowing the dog to show off an array of tricks and moves, which delight the crowd. This discipline demands a huge amount of training, but if rewards are on hand, and you keep it light-hearted, the Shar Pei may well surprise you!

Does your Shar Pei have what it takes to make it in the show ring?

Does your Shar Pei have what it takes to make it in the show ring?

|Health care

The Shar Pei has had a chequered history and indiscriminate breeding has allowed health conditions to creep in. However, if you buy a puppy from a responsible breeder, and pursue a programme of good care and management, including a preventative health regime, your Shar Pei will thrive.

Vaccinations

Dogs are subject to a number of contagious diseases. In the old days, these were killers, and resulted in heartbreak for many owners. Vaccinations have been developed, and the occurrence of the major infectious diseases is now very rare. However, this will only remain the case if all pet owners follow a strict policy of vaccinating their dogs.

There are vaccinations available for the following diseases:

Adenovirus: (Canine Adenovirus): This affects the liver; affected dogs have a classic 'blue eye'.

Distemper: A viral disease which causes chest and gastro-intestinal damage. The brain may also be affected, leading to fits and paralysis.

Parvovirus: Causes severe gastroenteritis, and most commonly affects puppies.

Leptospirosis: This bacterial disease is carried by rats and affects many mammals, including humans. It causes liver and kidney damage.

Rabies: A virus that affects the nervous system and is invariably fatal. The first signs are abnormal behaviour, when the infected dog may bite another animal or a person. Paralysis and death follow.

Vaccination is compulsory in most countries. In the UK, dogs travelling overseas must be vaccinated.

Kennel cough: There are several strains of Kennel Cough, but they all result in a harsh, dry, cough. This disease is rarely fatal; in fact most dogs make a good recovery within a matter of weeks and show few signs of ill health while they are affected. However, kennel cough is highly infectious among dogs that live together so, for this reason, most boarding kennels will insist that your dog is protected by the vaccine, which is given as nose drops.

Lyme disease: This is a bacterial disease transmitted by ticks (see page 167). The first signs are limping, but the heart, kidneys and nervous system can also be affected. The ticks that transmit the disease occur in specific regions, such as the north-east states of the USA, some of the southern states, California and the upper Mississippi region. Lyme disease is still rare in the UK so vaccinations are not routinely offered.

Vaccination programme

In the USA, the American Animal Hospital Association advises vaccination for core diseases, which they list as: distemper, adenovirus, parvovirus and rabies. The requirement for vaccinating for non-core diseases – leptospirosis, Lyme disease and Kennel cough – should be assessed depending on a dog's individual risk and his likely exposure to the disease. In the UK, vaccinations are routinely given for distemper, adenovirus, leptospirosis and parvovirus. In most cases, a puppy will start his vaccinations at around eight weeks of age, with the second part given a fortnight later.

However, this does vary depending on the individual policy of veterinary practices, and the incidence of disease in your area. You should also talk to your vet about whether to give annual booster vaccinations.

Parasites

No matter how well you look after your Shar Pei you will have to accept that parasites – internal and external – are ever present, and you need to take preventative action.

Internal parasites: As the name suggests, these parasites live inside your dog. Most will find a home in the digestive tract, but there is also a parasite that lives in the heart. If infestation is unchecked, a dog's health will be severely jeopardised, but routine preventative treatment is simple and effective.

External parasites: These parasites live on your dog's body – in his skin and fur, and sometimes in his ears.

Roundworm

This is found in the small intestine, and signs of infestation will be a poor coat, a pot-belly, diarrhoea and lethargy. Pregnant mothers should be treated, but it is almost inevitable that parasites will be passed on to the puppies.

For this reason, a breeder will start a worming programme, which you will need to continue. Ask your vet for advice on treatment, which will need to continue throughout your dog's life.

Tapeworm

Infection occurs when fleas and lice are ingested; the adult worm takes up residence in the small intestine, releasing mobile segments (which contain eggs) which can be seen in a dog's faeces as small rice-like grains. The only other obvious sign of infestation is irritation of the anus. Again, routine preventative treatment is required throughout your Shar Pei's life.

Heartworm

This parasite is transmitted by mosquitos, and so will only occur where these insects thrive. A warm environment is needed for the parasite to develop, so it is more likely to be present in areas with a warm, humid climate.

However, it is found in all parts of the USA, although its prevalence does vary. At present, heartworm is rarely seen in the UK. Heartworm live in the right side of the heart.

Larvae can grow up to 14 inches (35cm) in length. A dog with heartworm is at severe risk from heart failure, so preventative treatment, as advised by your vet, is essential. Dogs living in the USA should have regular blood tests to check for the presence of infection.

Lungworm

Lungworm, or *Angiostrongylus vasorum*, is a parasite that lives in the heart and major blood vessels supplying the lungs.

It can cause many problems, such as breathing difficulties, blood-clotting problems, sickness and diarrhoea, seizures, and can even be fatal.

The parasite is carried by slugs and snails, and the dog becomes infected when ingesting these, often

accidentally when rummaging through undergrowth. Lungworm is not common, but it is on the increase and a responsible owner should be aware of it.

Fortunately, it is easily preventable and even affected dogs usually make a full recovery if treated early enough. Your vet will be able to advise you on the risks in your area and what form of treatment may be required.

Fleas

A dog may carry dog fleas, cat fleas, and even human fleas. The flea stays on the dog only long enough to have a blood meal and to breed, but its presence will result in itching and scratching.

Preventative treatment needs be administered on a routine basis; this can be in the form of a tablet, spot-on treatment, an insecticidal spray or shampoo Ask your vet for advice on what product to use. Bear in mind that the whole environment your dog lives in will need to be sprayed, and all other pets living in your home will also need to be treated.

Spot-on treatment, which should be administered on a routine basis, is easy to use and highly effective on all types of fleas. You can also treat your dog with a spray or with insecticidal shampoo.

Bear in mind that the whole environment your dog lives in will need to be sprayed, and all other pets living in your home will also need to be treated.

How to detect fleas

You may suspect your dog has fleas, but how can you be sure? There are two methods to try.

Run a fine comb through your dog's coat, and see if you can detect the presence of fleas on the skin, or clinging to the comb. Alternatively, sit your dog on white paper and rub his back. This will dislodge faeces from the fleas, which will be visible as small brown specks. To double check, shake the specks on to damp cotton-wool (cotton). Flea faeces consists of the dried blood taken from the host, so if the specks turn a lighter shade of red, you know your dog has fleas.

Ticks

These are blood-sucking parasites, most frequently found in rural areas where sheep or deer are present. The main danger is their ability to pass lyme disease to both dogs and humans.

Lyme disease is prevalent in some areas of the USA (see page 161), although it is still rare in the UK.

The treatment you give your dog for fleas generally works for ticks, but it is a good idea to discuss the best product to use with your veterinary surgeon.

How to remove a tick

If you spot a tick on your dog, do not try to pluck it off as you risk leaving the hard mouth parts embedded in his skin. The best way to remove a tick is to use a fine pair of tweezers, or you can buy a tick remover. Grasp the tick head firmly and then pull the tick straight out from the skin. If you are using a tick remover, check the instructions, as some recommend a circular twist when pulling. When you have removed the tick, clean the area with mild soap and water.

Ear mites

These parasites live in the outer ear canal. The signs of infestation are a brown, waxy discharge, and your dog will continually shake his head and scratch his ear.

If you suspect your Shar Pei has ear mites, a visit to the vet will be needed so that medicated ear drops can be prescribed.

Fur mites

These small, white parasites are visible to the naked eye and are often referred to as 'walking dandruff'.

They cause a scurfy coat and mild itchiness. However, they are zoonetic, transferable to humans – so prompt treatment with an insecticide prescribed by your vet is essential.

Harvest mites

These are picked up from the undergrowth, and can be seen as a bright orange patch on the webbing between the toes, although this can be found elsewhere on the body, such as on the ear flaps.

Treatment is effective with the appropriate insecticide.

Skin mites

There are two types of parasite that burrow into a dog's skin.

Demodex canis is transferred from a mother to her pups while they are feeding. Treatment is with a topical preparation, and sometimes antibiotics are needed.

The other skin mite is *Sarcoptes scabiei*, which cause intense itching and hair loss.

It is highly contagious, so all dogs in a household will need to be treated, which involves repeated bathing with a medicated shampoo.

Common ailments

As with all living animals, dogs can be affected by a variety of ailments. Most can be treated effectively after consulting with your vet, who will prescribe appropriate medication and will advise you on how to care for your dog's needs.

Here are some of the more common problems that could affect your Shar Pei, with advice on how to deal with them.

Anal glands

These are two small sacs on either side of the anus, which produce a dark-brown secretion that dogs use when they mark their territory. The anal glands should empty every time a dog defecates but if they become blocked or impacted, a dog will experience increasing discomfort. He may nibble at his rear end, or 'scoot' his bottom along the ground to relieve the irritation. Treatment involves a trip to the vet, who will empty the glands manually. It is important to do this without delay or infection may occur.

Dental problems

Good dental hygiene will do much to minimise

gum infection and tooth decay, which is why teeth cleaning should be part of your regular care routine. If tartar accumulates to the extent that you cannot remove it by brushing, the vet will need to intervene. In a situation such as this, an anaesthetic will need to be administered so the tartar can be removed manually.

Diarrhoea

There are many reasons why a dog has diarrhoea, but most commonly it is the result of scavenging, a sudden change of diet, or an adverse reaction to a particular type of food.

If your dog is suffering from diarrhoea, the first step is to withdraw food for a day. It is important that he does not dehydrate, so make sure that fresh drinking water is available. However, drinking too much can increase the diarrhoea, which may be accompanied with vomiting, so limit how much he drinks at any one time.

After allowing the stomach to rest, feed a bland diet, such as white fish or chicken, with boiled rice for a few days. In most cases, your dog's motions will return to normal and you can resume normal feeding, although this should be done gradually. However, if this fails to work and the diarrhoea persists for more than a few days, you should consult your vet. Your dog may have an infection, which needs to be treated with antibiotics, or the diarrhoea may indicate some other problem, which needs expert diagnosis.

Ear infections

The Shar Pei has small ears in proportion to his head; they are set wide apart and the tips of the ears point towards the eyes. The problem with small ears is that it means narrow ear canals, which can be prone to infection. It is therefore essential to adopt a regular routine of ear cleaning to ensure your Shar Pei's ears are clean and healthy.

A healthy ear is clean with no sign of redness or inflammation, and no evidence of a waxy brown discharge or a foul odour. If you see your dog scratching his ear, shaking his head, or holding one ear at an odd angle, you will need to consult your vet.

The most likely causes are ear mites, an infection, or there may be a foreign body, such as a grass seed, trapped in the ear.

Depending on the cause, treatment is with medicated ear drops, possibly containing antibiotics. If a foreign body is suspected, the vet will need to carry out further investigations.

Keep a close check on your Shar Pei so you can spot any problems at an early stage.

Eye problems

The Shar Pei has small eyes, with wrinkling above the eye. Unfortunately, the desire to increase wrinkling has led to exaggeration so that the skin folds can adversely affect the eyes, causing irritation to the eyeball, as well as a predisposition to inherited conditions such as entropion (see page 183).

This type of exaggeration is now penalised in the show ring and responsible breeders no longer produce puppies of this type.

However, it is a problem you should be aware of, and you will need to keep a close check on your Shar Pei's eyes throughout his life.

If your Shar Pei eyes look red and sore, he is likely to be suffering from conjunctivitis. This may, or may not be accompanied with a watery or a crusty discharge.

Conjunctivitis can be caused by irritation to the eyeball which may be due to the dog's conformation (see above), a bacterial or viral infection, the result of an injury, or it could be an adverse reaction to pollen.

You will need to consult your vet for a correct diagnosis, but in the case of an infection, treatment with medicated eye drops is effective.

Conjunctivitis may also be the first sign of more serious inherited eye problems. In some instances, a dog may suffer from dry, itchy eye, which he may further injure through scratching. This condition, known as *Keratoconjunctivitis sicca*, may be inherited.

Foreign bodies

In the home, puppies – and some older dogs – cannot resist chewing anything that looks interesting. The toys you choose for your dog should be suitably robust to withstand damage, but children's toys can be irresistible.

Some dogs will chew – and swallow – anything from socks, tights, and any other items from the laundry basket to golf balls and stones from the garden.

Obviously, these items are indigestible and could cause an obstruction in your dog's intestine, which is potentially lethal.

The signs to look for are vomiting, and a tucked up posture.

The dog will often be restless and will look as though he is in pain.

In this situation, you must get your dog to the vet without delay, as surgery will be needed to remove the obstruction.

Heatstroke

The Shar Pei has a very unusual head structure, which means he is prone to respiratory problems and may struggle to regulate his body temperature in warm conditions. Many owners fail to appreciate that a dog may suffer from over-heating on warm days, and not just on days when the temperature soars.

This is particularly the case if your dog has undertaken rigorous exercise. If the weather is warm make sure your Shar Pei has access to shady areas, and wait for a cooler part of the day before going for a walk.

Be extra careful if you leave your Shar Pei in the car, as the temperature can rise dramatically - even on a cloudy day. Heatstroke can happen very rapidly, and unless you are able to lower your dog's temperature, it can be fatal.

If your Shar Pei appears to be suffering from heatstroke, lie him flat and work at lowering his temperature by spraying him with cool water and covering him with wet towels. As soon as he has made some recovery, take him to the vet where cold intravenous fluids can be administered.

For information on respiratory disease, see Brachycephalic Upper Airway Syndrome, page 182.

Lameness/ limping

There are a wide variety of reasons why a dog can go lame; from a simple muscle strain, to a fracture, ligament damage, or more complex problems with the joints. If you are concerned about your dog, do not delay in seeking help.

As your Shar Pei becomes more elderly, he may suffer from arthritis, which you will see as general stiffness, particularly when he gets up after resting.

It will help if you ensure his bed is in a warm draught-free location, and if your Shar Pei gets wet after exercise, you must dry him thoroughly. If your Shar Pei seems to be in pain, consult your vet who will be able to help with pain relief medication.

Skin problems

The Shar Pei has heavy skin folds and this means he is prone to skin problems. Most commonly, this will take the form of skinfold dermatitis which results in recurring bouts of skin irritation and soreness (see page 186). Fleas, and other external parasites can result in itching, and the skin can become very sore and inflamed if the dog has an allergic reaction. Food intolerance and environmental factors, such as dust mites or pollen, can also cause major skin problems.

For information on Allergies, see page 182.

Breed specific conditions

All pedigree dogs have a risk of inheriting a health condition from their parents or grandparents, and in some cases, the family history of disease may date back even further. There are also a number of conditions which are more likely to crop up in specific breeds because of their conformation.

The Shar Pei's unique appearance makes him vulnerable in terms of respiratory problems and skin conditions. There is also the fact that the breed has been developed from a relatively small gene pool which exacerbates problems with inherited conditions.

Responsible breeders are working hard to eradicate health problems from their breeding programmes, and the health of the breed is improving. However, it is important to be aware of conditions which may affect your Shar Pei.

Allergies

Allergies resulting in hair loss, itching and soreness are far from uncommon in the Shar Pei. The underlying cause may be diet or it could be due to environmental factors such as pollen or dust mites.

The solution is to find out what is triggering the allergy, for example, eliminating certain food from the diet, which is not always easy. In the meantime, creams and antihistamines can be used to alleviate the symptoms.

Brachycephalic upper airway syndrome

This is a respiratory condition that can affect any of the brachycephalic breeds, which share a flat-faced, short-nosed head structure. In warm conditions, they have difficulty breathing and therefore their cooling system does not function properly.

The soft tissue in the palate obscures the trachea and prevents air from flowing over the tongue, which is the way in which dogs cool down and lower their body temperature.

It is important to manage this condition by ensuring your Shar Pei does not get over-heated.

Eye conditions

The Shar Pei may be affected by two principal eye disorders:

Entropion

This is when the eyelids turn inwards and rub against the cornea of the eye causing irritation and sometimes ulceration.

The condition can be corrected with surgery. Dogs who have suffered from entropion should not be used for breeding, as there is a hereditary link. In some cases, evidence of entropion is detected as soon as puppies open their eyes at around 10 days. A pup will first open his eyes, but will then start squinting and will have difficulty opening them properly.

This may be accompanied by a mucous eye discharge. Treatment involves applying temporary sutures until corrective surgery can be undertaken at around six months of age.

Cherry Eye

This is a protrusion of the third eyelid, resulting in the gland for the third eyelid becoming detached.

It is seen as a round, red blob in the inner corner of the eye, and can sometimes become so big as to obscure the entire eye. The condition can be corrected with surgery.

Elbow dysplasia

This is an abnormality of the elbow joint, which causes pain and disability. Elbows should be X-rayed and scored before dogs are bred from.

Hip dysplasia

This is an abnormality of the ball and socket hip joint. The first signs are lameness, and the condition can deteriorate rapidly depending on the extent of the dysplasia.

Again, potential breeding stock should be X-rayed and scored.

Hypothyroidism

This condition is caused by a malfunctioning thyroid gland. Signs of the disease include: lethargy, becoming overweight on a normal diet, hair loss, skin changes, including scaly skin and increased pigmentation.

Secondary skin infections may follow, often accompanied by discharge from the ears and subsequent infection. Blood tests will determine the thyroid function and administration of the thyroid hormone is used to treat the condition.

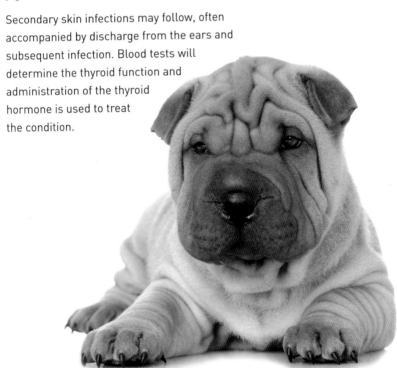

Shar Pei fever

This is condition, also known as Swollen Hock Syndrome, affects the autoimmune system.

A recurring fever is accompanied by swollen and aching joints; the hock joint is most commonly affected. It is estimated that one in five victims go on to develop Amyloidosis, which involves chronic inflammation of the kidneys and liver, and can be fatal.

Skin conditions

There are a number of skin disorders which may affect the Shar Pei:

Skinfold Dermatitis

This affects a number of breeds that have wrinkles, and the Shar Pei is therefore a prime candidate for this condition.

It is caused by warm, moist conditions deep in the skin and results in hair loss, bad odour, soreness and irritation. If untreated it can develop into an infection known as pyoderma.

Cutaneous Mucinosis

Mucin is a clear, stringy substance which causes wrinkling in the Shar Pei. If an excess of this substance is produced, it may be seen as clear

bubbles on the skin which rupture and ooze. It most commonly occurs on the neck, forelimbs, hocks and anus. Treatment with steroid medication is effective.

Seborrhea Oleosa

This will be detected as rancid body odour, which comes from raw, scaly, or bloody skin. It could be caused by hypothyroidism (see page 185), yeast infections, or it can be an allergic reaction. Consult your vet for treatment with shampoos and medication.

Summing up

It may give the pet owner cause for concern to find about health problems that may affect their dog.

But it is important to bear in mind that acquiring some basic knowledge is an asset, as it will allow you to spot signs of trouble at an early stage. Early diagnosis is very often the means to the most effective treatment.

Good care and management are key, and will enable you to spend many happy years with this most loyal and distinguished companion.

Useful addresses

Breed & Kennel Clubs

Please contact your Kennel Club to obtain contact information about breed clubs in your area.

UK

The Kennel Club (UK)
1 Clarges Street London, W1J 8AB
Telephone: 0870 606 6750
Fax: 0207 518 1058
Web: www.thekennelclub.org.uk

USA

American Kennel Club (AKC)
5580 Centerview Drive, Raleigh, NC 27606.
Telephone: 919 233 9767
Fax: 919 233 3627
Email: info@akc.org
Web: www.akc.org

United Kennel Club (UKC)
100 E Kilgore Rd, Kalamazoo,
MI 49002-5584, USA.
Tel: 269 343 9020
Fax: 269 343 7037
Web: www.ukcdogs.com

Australia

Australian National Kennel Council (ANKC)
The Australian National Kennel Council is the administrative body for pure breed canine affairs in Australia. It does not, however, deal directly with dog exhibitors, breeders or judges. For information pertaining to breeders, clubs or shows, please contact the relevant State or Territory Body.

International

Fédération Cynologique Internationalé (FCI)
Place Albert 1er, 13, B-6530 Thuin, Belgium.
Tel: +32 71 59.12.38
Fax: +32 71 59.22.29
Web: www.fci.be

Training and behavior

UK

Association of Pet Dog Trainers
Telephone: 01285 810811
Web: www.apdt.co.uk

Canine Behaviour
Association of Pet Behaviour Counsellors
Telephone: 01386 751151
Web: www.apbc.org.uk

USA

Association of Pet Dog Trainers
Tel: 1 800 738 3647
Web: www.apdt.com

American College of Veterinary Behaviorists
Web: dacvb.org

American Veterinary Society of Animal Behavior
Web: www.avsabonline.org

Australia

APDT Australia Inc
Web: www.apdt.com.au

For details of regional behaviorists, contact the relevant State or Territory Controlling Body.

Activities

UK

Agility Club
www.agilityclub.co.uk

British Flyball Association
Telephone: 01628 829623
Web: www.flyball.org.uk

USA

North American Dog Agility Council
Web: www.nadac.com

North American Flyball Association, Inc.
Tel/Fax: 800 318 6312
Web: www.flyball.org

Australia

Agility Dog Association of Australia
Tel: 0423 138 914
Web: www.adaa.com.au

NADAC Australia
Web: www.nadacaustralia.com

Australian Flyball Association
Tel: 0407 337 939
Web: www.flyball.org.au

International

World Canine Freestyle Organisation
Tel: (718) 332-8336
Web: www.worldcaninefreestyle.org

Health

UK

British Small Animal Veterinary Association
Tel: 01452 726700
Web: www.bsava.com

Royal College of Veterinary Surgeons
Tel: 0207 222 2001
Web: www.rcvs.org.uk

www.dogbooksonline.co.uk/healthcare

Alternative Veterinary Medicine Centre
Tel: 01367 710324
Web: www.alternativevet.org

USA

American Veterinary Medical Association
Tel: 800 248 2862
Web: www.avma.org

American College of Veterinary Surgeons
Tel: 301 916 0200
Toll Free: 877 217 2287
Web: www.acvs.org

Canine Eye Registration Foundation
The Veterinary Medical DataBases
1717 Philo Rd, PO Box 3007,
Urbana, IL 61803-3007
Tel: 217-693-4800
Fax: 217-693-4801
Web: www.vmdb.org/cerf.html

Orthopaedic Foundation of Animals
2300 E Nifong Boulevard
Columbia, Missouri, 65201-3806
Tel: 573 442-0418
Fax: 573 875-5073
Web: www.offa.org

American Holistic Veterinary Medical
Association
Tel: 410 569 0795
Web: www.ahvma.org

Australia

Australian Small Animal Veterinary
Association
Tel: 02 9431 5090
Web: www.asava.com.au

Australian Veterinary Association
Tel: 02 9431 5000
Web: www.ava.com.au

Australian College Veterinary Scientists
Tel: 07 3423 2016
Web: acvsc.org.au

Australian Holistic Vets
Web: www.ahv.com.au